PEANUTS

It's a Dog's Life, Snoopy

It's a Big World, Charlie Brown

BY CHARLES M. SCHULZ

Ballantine Books * New York

A Ballantine Book
Published by The Random House Publishing Group

Originally published in two separate volumes as:

It's a Dog's Life, Snoopy, Copyright © 2001 by United Feature Syndicate, Inc.
It's a Big World, Charlie Brown, Copyright © 2001 by United Feature Syndicate, Inc.

This edition is published in the United States by Ballantine Books, an imprint of The Random House Publishing Group,
a division of Random House, Inc., New York, and simultaneously in Canada by Random House of Canada Limited, Toronto.
The comic strips in this book were originally published in newspapers worldwide.

www.ballantinebooks.com
www.snoopy.com

ISBN: 978-0-307-29133-2

Printed in China in 2008

10 9 8 7 6 5 4 3 2

Contents

IT'S A DOG'S LIFE, SNOOPY

BY CHARLES M. SCHULZ

It's a Dog's Life,
SNOOPY

AND NO LOVE LETTERS CAME TUMBLING OUT..

1-5-98

BOY, THE SNOW IS COMING DOWN HEAVIER THAN EVER..

WHAT WE NEED IS SOMEONE TO GO OUT TO THE MAILBOX...

1-6-98

SOMEONE WHO DOESN'T MAKE A BIG DEAL OUT OF EVERYTHING..

AND STOP YELLING!

I WASN'T YELLING..I NEVER SAID A WORD..

1-7-98

STOP NEVER SAYING A WORD!

6

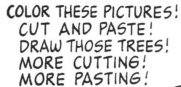

© 1998 United Feature Syndicate, Inc.

1-11

THIS IS A HARD TEST..

1-12

THIS ISN'T A TEST, SIR.. THEY JUST WANT TO KNOW WHEN YOU WERE BORN..

TOO LATE..I ALREADY PUT DOWN 1492!

AND THEY SAY NO TWO SNOWFLAKES ARE EVER ALIKE..

1-13

THAT'S RIDICULOUS.. I'VE SEEN FOUR ALREADY THIS MORNING THAT WERE EXACTLY ALIKE...

THEY WERE EVEN THE SAME COLOR!

HELLO?

HI, SALLY..THIS IS PATRICIA..I'M CALLING ABOUT A SCHOOL DANCE..

1-14

I DON'T SUPPOSE CHUCK WOULD GO WITH ME, WOULD HE? NO, I SUPPOSE NOT..

ANYWAY, TELL HIM I WAS THINKING OF HIM..

YOU ALMOST WENT TO A SCHOOL DANCE..

IS CHARLES HOME? I CAME OVER TO ASK HIM TO GO TO A SCHOOL DANCE..

I DOUBT IF HE'D EVER GO WITH SOMEONE LIKE ME, THOUGH, SO I WON'T BOTHER HIM..

FOR SOMEBODY WHO NEVER GOES ANYPLACE, YOU LEAD A VERY ACTIVE LIFE..

1-15

PATTY? THIS IS CHARLIE BROWN.. I HEAR YOU WANTED TO INVITE ME TO A SCHOOL DANCE..

THE DANCE WAS LAST NIGHT, CHUCK.. MAYBE NEXT YEAR, HUH?

1-16

NEXT YEAR FOR SURE.. SAVE ME THE WALTZ

"SAVE ME THE WALTZ"?

YOU'RE PRETTY SMOOTH, BIG BROTHER..

IT'S EASY TO BE SMOOTH WHEN YOU'RE OFF THE HOOK..

1-17
HOW DID THINGS GO IN COURT TODAY?

I ASKED THE JUDGE IF I COULD APPROACH THE BENCH..

HE SAID, "NO!" HE SAID I SHOULD STAY IN THE BACK YARD..

10

PEANUTS
by
SCHULZ

CHARLIE BROWN! TELL YOUR DOG TO STOP STARING AT ME!

IF YOU'LL SHARE WHATEVER YOU'RE EATING, MAYBE HE'LL GO AWAY..

© 1998 United Feature Syndicate, Inc.

www.unitedmedia.com

1-18

YOU AGAIN?

HOW DID YOU KNOW IT WAS ME?

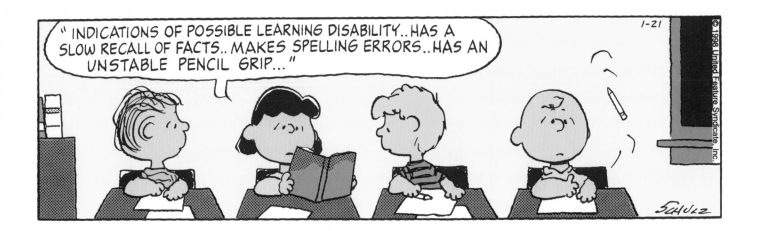

AND IT SAYS THE ANDROMEDA GALAXY IS SPEEDING TOWARD OUR GALAXY AT 300,000 MILES PER HOUR..

© 1998 United Feature Syndicate, Inc.

www.unitedmedia.com

1-22

I HEARD THE COYOTES HOWLING AGAIN LAST NIGHT, CHARLIE BROWN..

© 1998 United Feature Syndicate, Inc.

1/23

THAT'S THE LONELIEST SOUND IN THE WORLD..

LIKE A TRAIN WHISTLE AT MIDNIGHT..

OR A LONE CAN OPENER..

1-24

www.unitedmedia.com

© 1998 United Feature Syndicate, Inc.

13

WHOOPS! I FORGOT THE PARSLEY

I GOT THE PARSLEY.. WHOOPS! NOW I FORGOT YOUR DINNER!

WAIT A MINUTE.. THIS ISN'T YOUR DINNER..THIS IS MY DINNER!

I'LL BE RIGHT BACK..

1-25

OKAY, HERE WE GO..

?

IT WAS PRETTY GOOD ALTHOUGH IT COULD HAVE USED SOME PARSLEY..

IT'S TOO BAD YOU'RE NOT A HAWK..

SOME PEOPLE BELIEVE THAT HAWKS HAVE "ACCESS TO THE HEAVENS"

1-29

WELL, YES.. ACCESS TO THE MALL IS PRETTY GOOD..

SOMEONE AT SCHOOL TODAY ASKED ME IF I HAD AN OLDER BROTHER WHO DRAGGED A BLANKET AROUND.."NO," I REPLIED, "I'M AN ONLY CHILD!" THEN SOMEONE SAID, "BUT DON'T YOU HAVE A WEIRD OLDER SISTER?" "NO," I INSISTED, "I'M AN ONLY CHILD!" AND SO I GO, DAY AFTER DAY, DODGING QUESTIONS FROM CURIOUS OUTSIDERS..

1-30

I HAVE TO DO A REPORT ON CLOUDS..

WHAT KIND OF CLOUDS?

I DON'T KNOW..YOU TELL ME..

HOW ABOUT RAIN CLOUDS?

THAT'S GOOD.. HERE, YOU WRITE IT..

I CAN'T DO YOUR HOMEWORK FOR YOU..

I HOPE IT RAINS ON YOU

1-31

JUST BECAUSE YOU'RE SMALL, YOU DON'T ALWAYS HAVE TO BE AFRAID..

LEARN TO FIGHT BACK! DON'T LET ANYONE PUSH YOU AROUND!

2-2

IF YOU'RE THE THIRD CHILD IN A FAMILY, AND YOUR BROTHER AND SISTER ARE DEFINITELY WEIRD, I WONDER IF IT'S POSSIBLE FOR THAT THIRD CHILD TO DEVELOP AN IMMUNITY TO ALL THE UNFORTUNATE THINGS THAT OCCUR IN A FAMILY TO THAT INNOCENT THIRD CHILD WHO...

SO MUCH FOR IMMUNITY..

2-3

CAN A PIANO PLAYER SUPPORT A WIFE WHO IS USED TO ALL THE NICE THINGS IN LIFE?

2-4

YOU KNOW, CARS, CLOTHES, A BEACH HOUSE.. THINGS LIKE THAT..

ABSOLUTELY! PIANO PLAYERS MAKE ENORMOUS AMOUNTS OF MONEY! THEIR WIVES CAN BUY ANYTHING THEY WANT!

I'LL PROBABLY MARRY A VIOLA PLAYER..

TELL MY SWEET BABBOO I'M HERE TO PICK UP MY VALENTINE..

I'M NOT HER SWEET BABBOO, AND I WOULDN'T GIVE HER A VALENTINE IF SHE WERE THE LAST PERSON ON EARTH!

WAIT HERE..I'LL GO KICK HIM FOR YOU..

OW!

THANK YOU.. NO PROBLEM.. THAT'S WHAT SISTERS ARE FOR..

WHAT ARE YOU WRITING, MARCIE?

I'M SENDING A VALENTINE TO CHARLES YOU CAN'T DO THAT..HE'LL THINK YOU LIKE HIM..

I DO..I'M VERY FOND OF CHARLES WHY DON'T YOU SIGN MY NAME, TOO?

OH, SURE! HITCH A RIDE ON MY VALENTINE!

HI, CHARLES..DID YOU LIKE OUR VALENTINE?

YES, THANK YOU..IT WAS NICE NICE?

HE SAID IT WAS "NICE".. ASK HIM IF WE CAN HAVE IT BACK..

THE DAY ISN'T OVER.. WE CAN STILL GIVE IT TO SOMEONE ELSE..

22

PEANUTS by Schulz

WELL, HOW DOES OUR BALL FIELD LOOK THIS YEAR, CHARLIE BROWN?

2-15

I THINK OUR GROUNDSKEEPER IS DOING A GOOD JOB..

THE INFIELD LOOKS GREAT AND THE GRASS IN THE OUTFIELD HAS NEVER LOOKED BETTER..

I THINK IT'S BECAUSE WE HAVE A NEW AUTOMATIC SPRINKLER SYSTEM...

♪

24

BONK!

AND THEN I THREW THE BALL SO HARD, IT FLEW CLEAR AROUND THE WORLD AND BACK AGAIN, AND HIT ME ON THE HEAD!

WHAT ARE YOU LAUGHING AT?!

27

GRAMPA WISHES HE HAD HIS OLD CAR BACK..

WHEN THE MILEAGE MADE A BIG CHANGE, IT WAS FUN TO WATCH ALL THE NUMBERS ON THE ODOMETER ROLL UP..

HE SAYS THAT WAS HIS FAVORITE PROGRAM..

2-26

WHEN YOU'RE A PUPPY, ONE OF THE FIRST THINGS THEY TEACH YOU IS TO "SHAKE HANDS"

2-27

THEN YOU KNOW WHAT MOM ALWAYS SAID?

MAKE SURE YOU WASH YOUR PAWS AFTERWARD..

I THOUGHT YOU WERE GOING OUTSIDE..

I CAN'T..THEY SAID TO STAY TUNED FOR SCENES FROM NEXT WEEK'S EPISODE..

WELL, I'M GOING OUTSIDE..

I'D SURE LIKE TO GO WITH YOU..

I HAVE TO STAY TUNED FOR SCENES FROM NEXT WEEK'S EPISODE..

2-28

 FLY, YOU STUPID KITE! GET UP THERE! GO!

 FLY! FLY! GET UP THERE! GET UP THERE!

 YOU STUPID KITE! WHAT'S WRONG WITH YOU?! YOU'RE A DISGRACE TO KITEDOM!

 DON'T THINK YOU CAN GET AWAY WITH THIS! GET BACK UP THERE WHERE YOU BELONG!!

 HOW DID YOUR KITE FLYING GO TODAY? WELL I THINK I LEARNED SOMETHING, BUT I'M NOT SURE WHAT IT WAS..

29

ALL RIGHT, I DON'T HAVE TO REMIND YOU HOW IMPORTANT THIS GAME IS TODAY...

REMIND ME ANYWAY..

3-2

THIS GAME TODAY IS VERY IMPORTANT!

THANKS FOR REMINDING ME!

© 1998 United Feature Syndicate, Inc.

www.unitedmedia.com

HEY, MANAGER! HOW COME I ALWAYS HAVE TO PLAY RIGHT FIELD?

BECAUSE YOU'RE NOT ONLY THE WORST PLAYER ON OUR TEAM, YOU'RE ALSO THE WORST PLAYER IN THE HISTORY OF THE GAME!

www.unitedmedia.com

YOU LOOK LIKE YOU'VE BEEN GAINING A LITTLE WEIGHT..

3-3

© 1998 United Feature Syndicate, Inc.

HEY, MANAGER..

NOW WHAT?

WE HAD TORTELLINI FOR DINNER LAST NIGHT..

3-4

SOME OF IT WAS WHITE, SOME GREEN, AND SOME KIND OF ORANGE..ISN'T THAT SOMETHING?

HOW'S THE GAME GOING?

© 1998 United Feature Syndicate, Inc.

www.unitedmedia.com

31

HE'S MELTING! QUICK! DIAL "NINE-ONE-ONE"!

THE "NINE" LOOKS LIKE A SMALL "ZERO" WITH A TAIL..

3-8

WOOF!

IT'S TOO LATE.. CANCEL THE CALL

WOOF!

I'M PRACTICING MY QUESTION MARKS.. QUESTION MARKS ARE IMPORTANT IN CASE YOU HAVE TO SAY..

WHAT?

3-9

© 1998 United Feature Syndicate, Inc.

www.unitedmedia.com

SCHULZ

NO, THANKS.. I'M WITH HIM, AND HE'S JUST LOOKING..

3-10

© 1998 United Feature Syndicate, Inc.

SCHULZ

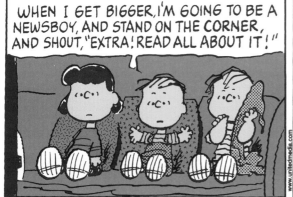

WHEN I GET BIGGER, I'M GOING TO BE A NEWSBOY, AND STAND ON THE CORNER, AND SHOUT, "EXTRA! READ ALL ABOUT IT!"

"LINDBERGH FLIES ACROSS THE OCEAN!"

THAT'S RIGHT..

YOU NEED A BLANKET LIKE YOUR BROTHER!

© 1998 United Feature Syndicate, Inc.

www.unitedmedia.com

3/11

SCHULZ

I'VE BEEN THINKING OF TAKING A SPECIAL COURSE IN FRENCH..

MAYBE EVEN A LITTLE LATIN AND SOME SPANISH.. WHAT DO YOU THINK?

"D-MINUS" SPOKEN HERE..

3-12

NO, MA'AM.. I DON'T KNOW THE ANSWER..

3-13

ACTUALLY, I DON'T KNOW ANYTHING..

I'M JUST HERE TO DRESS THE SET..

I'M ALWAYS CURIOUS ABOUT STRATEGY

WHEN YOU AND YOUR OPPONENT COME TO THE LAST HOLE, AND YOU'RE TIED, WHAT'S YOUR STRATEGY?

HOPE HE HITS IT IN THE WATER..

3-14

© 1998 United Feature Syndicate, Inc.

34

35

SOMETIMES I LIE AWAKE AT NIGHT, AND I WORRY, AND WORRY, AND WORRY...

THEN A VOICE COMES TO ME OUT OF THE DARK THAT SAYS, "WE UNDERSTAND YOUR PROBLEM..DETAILS AT ELEVEN"

3-16

© 1998 United Feature Syndicate, Inc.

THIS IS A HOE..

YES, I'VE SEEN PICTURES..

EVERY PERSON IN THIS WORLD WHO HAS EVER AMOUNTED TO SOMETHING STARTED BY USING A HOE!

3-17

SUDDENLY, I'M ON THE ROAD TO GREATNESS..

© 1998 United Feature Syndicate, Inc.

THIS IS GOING TO BE OUR GARDEN..

SO?

SO YOUR JOB IS TO TAKE THAT HOE AND DIG OUT ALL THE WEEDS AND ROCKS..

3-18

I CAN DO THAT..WHEN DO YOU WANT IT FINISHED?

THIS AFTERNOON

I WAS THINKING MORE LIKE MAYBE IN FIFTY YEARS..

© 1998 United Feature Syndicate, Inc.

36

THIS HOEING IS HARD WORK.. I'M NOT GETTING ANYWHERE..

THAT'S BECAUSE YOU'RE HOEING ON THE SIDEWALK.. YOU'RE SUPPOSED TO HOE IN THE YARD..

3-19

MY MOTHER DIDN'T RAISE ME TO BE A FARMER!

I SEE YOU'VE GOT RERUN OUT THERE WORKING WITH A HOE..

IT'S GOOD FOR HIM.. ALL GREAT PEOPLE GOT THEIR START WORKING WITH A HOE..

3-20

HERE'S TIGER WOODS HITTING A 3-WOOD TO THE EIGHTEENTH GREEN..

I CHANGED MY MIND.. I DECIDED I DON'T WANT A GARDEN..

WHAT ABOUT ALL THE WEEDS I DUG UP?

PUT 'EM BACK WHERE THEY WERE..

3-21

I SHOULD HAVE NUMBERED THEM..

"SLEEP TIGHT.. DON'T LET THE BEDBUGS BITE"

OKAY, BRING IN THE SHEEP..

ONE, TWO, THREE, FOUR, FIVE...

A GOAT! WHERE DID THAT GOAT COME FROM?

© 1998 United Feature Syndicate, Inc.

3-22

GEESE! WHO LET IN ALL THOSE GEESE? THERE'S ANOTHER GOAT! WHO LET IN THE GOATS? AND THAT HORSE! WHERE DID THAT HORSE COME FROM?!

BAM! BAM! BAM!

SOMETIMES WHEN I HAVE TROUBLE GOING TO SLEEP, I COUNT SHEEP..

TWENTY-FIVE SHEEP, TWO GOATS, FOURTEEN GEESE, A HORSE, AND I'M STILL AWAKE!

www.unitedmedia.com

SCHULZ

WELL, TIME FOR SCHOOL AGAIN..

I GUESS THAT DOESN'T MEAN MUCH TO YOU..YOUR LIFE IS MORE SIMPLE..

EDUCATION ISN'T THAT IMPORTANT..

ANYWAY, I'LL SEE YOU LATER..

AU REVOIR

3-23

HERE'S THE WORLD WAR I FLYING ACE WALKING OUT ONTO THE AERODROME..

AS HE SETTLES INTO THE COCKPIT OF HIS SOPWITH CAMEL, HE SURVEYS THE DARKENING SKY..LIGHTNING FLASHES IN THE EAST..

ONLY THE BRAVEST AND MOST DEDICATED PILOT WOULD FLY IN WEATHER LIKE THIS..

LOOK AT THIS CUTE PICTURE OF A BOY AND HIS DOG IN FRONT OF A FIREPLACE..

WHERE'D HE GET A DOG LIKE THAT?

3/24

ASK YOUR DOG IF HE WANTS TO GO OVER TO THE PARK AND PLAY..

3-25

WILL THEY BE GIVING OUT AWARDS?

EVERYBODY IN THE WORLD HAS A DOG.. WHY WON'T MOM LET ME HAVE A DOG?

A LOT OF PEOPLE IN THE WORLD DON'T HAVE DOGS..

WHY WON'T MOM LET THEM HAVE A DOG?

3-26

WHAT I THINK I'LL DO TODAY IS TAKE SOME MONEY OUT OF MY COLLEGE TRUST FUND, AND GO BUY A DOG..

YOU DON'T HAVE A COLLEGE TRUST FUND

I DON'T?

3-27

PLEASE PASS THE GRAPE JELLY..

WE'RE ALL OUT OF GRAPE JELLY..

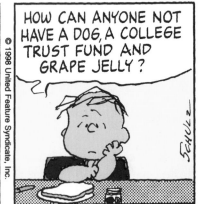

HOW CAN ANYONE NOT HAVE A DOG, A COLLEGE TRUST FUND AND GRAPE JELLY?

SO THE FAMILY GOES INTO THE MALL, AND I'M LEFT ALONE IN THE CAR...

HERE'S THE WORLD FAMOUS BIG-RIG OPERATOR TOOLING HIS WAY TOWARD OMAHA..

ONE MINUTE HERE WHILE WE TAKE THE MAP OUT OF THE GLOVE COMPARTMENT..

3/28

ONE MINUTE HERE WHILE WE TRY TO GET THE MAP BACK INTO THE GLOVE COMPARTMENT..

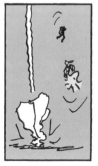

ONE HUNDRED AND ONE.. ONE HUNDRED AND TWO.. ONE HUNDRED AND THREE...

HOW MUCH IS THAT IN DOG YEARS?

YES, MA'AM..REQUEST PERMISSION TO GO OUT FOR A DRINK OF WATER..

YES, MA'AM..REQUEST PERMISSION TO COPY ALL THE ANSWERS FROM MARCIE'S PAPER WHILE SHE'S OUT OF THE ROOM..

I'M BACK.. WHY IS THE TEACHER FROWNING?

I DON'T KNOW..SHE FROWNS A LOT..

"APRIL FOOL!"

YOU DON'T SAY "APRIL FOOL" UNTIL YOU SAY SOMETHING ELSE FIRST..

WHAT SHOULD I SAY?

SAY ANYTHING YOU WANT

THIS IS TOO HARD..

44

WHY DO DOGS EAT SO FAST?

WE HAVE TO EAT FAST BEFORE THE HYENAS COME TO TRY TO TAKE AWAY THE KILL..

INCIDENTALLY, IF YOU'RE WORRIED ABOUT HYENAS, THERE AREN'T ANY AROUND HERE..

DID YOU LOOK IN THE TREES?

© 1998 United Feature Syndicate, Inc.

4-6

SOME KID OVER AT THE PLAYGROUND PUSHED ME OFF THE SWING..I WANT YOU TO TEACH HIM A LESSON..

WHERE IS HE NOW?

© 1998 United Feature Syndicate, Inc.

4/7

HERE..I BROUGHT HIM HOME SO YOU CAN HIT HIM..

HERE, TEACH THIS KID A LESSON! HE PUSHED ME OFF THE SWING.. I'LL HOLD HIM WHILE YOU HIT HIM!

I CAN'T HIT A LITTLE KID LIKE THAT..

TELL YOUR DOG TO BITE HIM..

© 1998 United Feature Syndicate, Inc.

4-8

45

HE PUSHED ME OFF THE SWING..TEACH HIM A LESSON..HIT HIM!

DID YOU REALLY PUSH HER OFF THE SWING?

IT WAS A MISTAKE..I THOUGHT SHE WAS MY SISTER..

4-9

FIRST HE PUSHES ME OFF THE SWING, THEN HE SAYS HE THINKS I'M CUTE..

4-10

IF SOMEONE TELLS YOU YOU'RE CUTE WHEN YOU KNOW YOU'RE NOT CUTE, WHAT DO YOU DO?

NEVER MIND.. I ALREADY KNOW

STUPID KID!!

I HATE TO TELL YOU, BUT DINNER WILL BE A LITTLE LATE TONIGHT..

ACTUALLY, I'M NOT SURE JUST HOW LATE..MAYBE TEN MINUTES..MAYBE TWO MINUTES..MAYBE THREE SECONDS..

ANYWAY, JUST SO YOU KNOW..

THREE SECONDS IS A LONG TIME..

4-11

46

47

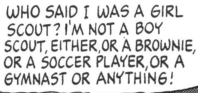

50

THIS IS MY REPORT ON WHAT'S HIS NAME..

HE WAS BORN SOMETIME BETWEEN SEVENTEEN AND EIGHTEEN HUNDRED.. VERY LITTLE IS KNOWN ABOUT HIM..

4-20

IN FACT, WE DON'T EVEN KNOW WHO HE WAS, OR SHE WAS, OR WHATEVER..

YES, MA'AM.. THANK YOU..

ANOTHER ONE OF THE GREAT REPORTS OF ALL TIME, SIR

GOING TO BE HARD TO FOLLOW, HUH, MARCIE?

© 1998 United Feature Syndicate, Inc.

"WHO LEFT THE DOOR OPEN?" THAT'S MY NEW PHILOSOPHY..

www.snoopy.com

I'M SURE IT WILL BE A GREAT SOURCE OF COMFORT DURING TIMES OF STRESS..

4-21

© 1998 United Feature Syndicate, Inc.

I SEE YOU USED ALL THE MILK AGAIN..

WHO LEFT THE DOOR OPEN?

HERE'S THE WORLD WAR I FLYING ACE HOME ON LEAVE..

4-22

www.snoopy.com

IT'S NICE TO BE BACK AMONG OLD FRIENDS WHERE YOU'RE APPRECIATED..

© 1998 United Feature Syndicate, Inc.

PLEASE TAKE YOUR ROOT BEER GLASS OFF MY PIANO..

SCHULZ

HERE'S THE WORLD WAR I FLYING ACE HOME ON LEAVE..

HOW GOOD IT IS TO BE FAR FROM THE FRONT LINES

HOW GOOD IT IS TO BE BACK IN THE PEACEFUL COUNTRYSIDE AGAIN..

IF YOU'RE NOT PLAYING, GET OFF THE FIELD!

4-23

HEY, CHARLES..MOM SAYS TO COME GET YOUR DOG..

HE'S IN OUR KITCHEN AGAIN DRINKING ROOT BEER.... ALL RIGHT, I'LL TELL HIM..

GENERAL PERSHING JUST CALLED..ALL LEAVES HAVE BEEN CANCELED..YOU'RE TO GET BACK TO THE AERODROME IMMEDIATELY!

WITH OR WITHOUT A KISS?

4-24

WITHOUT..

I DON'T UNDERSTAND YOU..

YOU CAN'T JUST WALK INTO SOMEONE'S KITCHEN, AND START DRINKING ROOT BEER!

WHAT IF THEY DON'T WANT YOU? IT'S NOT AS IF YOU WERE INVITED! THERE ARE SOME THINGS YOU JUST DON'T DO!

4-25

WAS HE TALKING TO ME?

HERE'S THE WORLD FAMOUS AUTHOR ON HIS WAY TO MAIL HIS LATEST NOVEL TO THE PUBLISHER..

!

I DIDN'T KNOW MAILBOXES COULD RUN..

SOMEDAY I'M GOING TO BE SIX FEET TALL, AND EVERYONE WILL RESPECT ME

GOOD FOR YOU..

IS SIX FEET VERY HIGH?

WHAT'S THIS?

I SUPPOSE YOU THINK IT'S SUPPERTIME..

NO, I ALWAYS WALK AROUND WITH A DISH IN MY MOUTH..

55

DO YOU THINK IT'S A BROTHER'S DUTY TO HELP HIS SISTER WITH HER HOMEWORK IF SHE'S HAVING TROUBLE?

YES, I SHOULD THINK SO..

GOOD

5-4

DUTY CALLS!

I TOLD MY TEACHER HOW YOU HELPED ME WITH MY HOMEWORK LAST NIGHT..

SHE SAID YOU GOT ALL THE ANSWERS WRONG..

SHE ASKED ME WHAT WE SHOULD DO ABOUT YOU...

5-5

I SUGGESTED LIFE IMPRISONMENT WITHOUT POSSIBILITY OF PAROLE..

YES, MA'AM, I HELPED MY SISTER WITH HER HOMEWORK

WE GOT ALL THE ANSWERS WRONG? HOW COULD THAT BE?

5-6

ANYWAY, I DID MY BEST.. I TRIED TO HELP HER...

ISN'T THERE MORE TO LIFE THAN GETTING THE ANSWERS RIGHT?

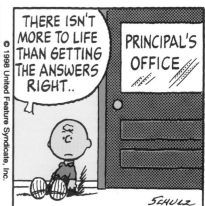

THERE ISN'T MORE TO LIFE THAN GETTING THE ANSWERS RIGHT..

PRINCIPAL'S OFFICE

"I will always wait for you," she said.
"I'm not going anyplace," he said.

"If you don't go anyplace, I can't wait for you," she said.

THAT'S THE DUMBEST THING I'VE EVER READ!

I'LL ADD SOME FOOTNOTES..

5-7

THOSE ARE NICE SHOES, RERUN..

THEY FEEL GOOD..

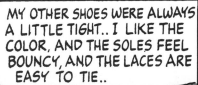

MY OTHER SHOES WERE ALWAYS A LITTLE TIGHT.. I LIKE THE COLOR, AND THE SOLES FEEL BOUNCY, AND THE LACES ARE EASY TO TIE..

WHEN YOU GET A COMPLIMENT, ALL YOU HAVE TO SAY IS, "THANK YOU"

I'M SORRY...I'VE NEVER HAD A COMPLIMENT BEFORE

5-8

I KNOW THE SONG, BUT WHAT WAS IT CALLED?

I KNOW HIS NAME, BUT I CAN'T REMEMBER IT..

I KNOW WHERE THAT IS, BUT I CAN'T REMEMBER WHERE..

I KNOW WHO SAID THAT, BUT I CAN'T THINK WHO IT WAS..

5-9
I SHOULD BE ON THAT PROGRAM BECAUSE I KNOW ALL THE ANSWERS..

58

PEANUTS by Schulz

THIS IS MY FAVORITE TIME OF YEAR... I THINK..

"TRICK OR TREAT!"

"TRICK OR TREAT"? THIS ISN'T HALLOWEEN!

DON'T YOU KNOW WHAT MONTH THIS IS? DON'T YOU HAVE A CALENDAR?

I'M JUST A LITTLE KID.. I DON'T KNOW HOW TO READ A CALENDAR! I DON'T EVEN KNOW WHAT DAY THIS IS! NOBODY TELLS ME ANYTHING!

5-10

ALL RIGHT..HERE'S A CANDY BAR..HAPPY HALLOWEEN..

THANK YOU

BY THE WAY, JUST SO YOU KNOW, TODAY IS MOTHER'S DAY..

IT IS?

HOW MANY DAYS 'TIL CHRISTMAS?

HEY, CHUCK.. YOU WANNA GO WITH ME?

GO WHERE?

DON'T YOU KNOW ANYTHING, CHUCK?

YOU'D BETTER BE THERE! AND DON'T FORGET, I ASKED YOU BEFORE WHAT'S-HER-NAME DID!

WHO WAS THAT?

I'VE BEEN INVITED TO SOMETHING SOMEPLACE BEFORE WHAT'S-HER-NAME INVITES ME SOMETIME..

5-11

© 1998 United Feature Syndicate, Inc.

www.snoopy.com

IT'S THE SPRING DANCE, CHARLIE BROWN.. JUST THINK..YOU'LL BE ABLE TO DANCE WITH THE LITTLE RED-HAIRED GIRL..

YOU'LL TAKE HER SOFT, COOL, LITTLE HAND IN YOURS, AND...

5-12

KLUNK!

FELL RIGHT OUT OF THE DESK, MA'AM..

© 1998 United Feature Syndicate, Inc.

www.snoopy.com

IT'S THE SPRING DANCE, CHARLES.. WOULD YOU LIKE TO GO WITH ME?

WHO IS THIS?

SHE'S MARCIE, CHUCK, YOU BLOCKHEAD! YOU CAN'T GO WITH HER! YOU SAID YOU'D GO WITH ME!

I'M A BETTER DANCER, CHARLES..

DON'T PUSH THE ENVELOPE, CHUCK..

TANGO TANGO, CHARLES!

5-13

© 1998 United Feature Syndicate, Inc.

www.snoopy.com

60

AND WHEN YOU'RE DANCING WITH THE LITTLE RED-HAIRED GIRL, CHARLIE BROWN, SHE'LL LOOK INTO YOUR EYES...

AND SHE'LL SEE HOW YOU LOVE HER, AND HOW YOU WILL ALWAYS LOVE HER, AND...

5-14

KLUNK!

EVER GO TO DANCES, MA'AM?

5-15

HEY, CHUCK, WHEN WE GO TO THE DANCE, ARE YOU GONNA PICK ME UP IN A LIMO?

OR MAYBE WE SHOULD JUST MEET THERE, HUH, CHARLES?

5-16

MEET WHERE? WHO IS THIS?

IT'S US, CHUCK, YOU BLOCKHEAD!

I THINK YOU'VE GOT THOSE GIRLS ALL CONFUSED, BIG BROTHER..

I FORGOT TO TELL THEM TO SAVE ME THE WALTZ..

C'MON, ROY! YOU CAN DO IT!

WHAT ARE YOU WATCHING?

"THE NATURAL".. I'M WAITING FOR MY FAVORITE SCENE..

THIS IS WHERE ROY HOBBS HITS A HOME RUN IN THE NINTH INNING..THE BALL SMASHES INTO THE LIGHTS, AND SPARKS FLY ALL OVER THE FIELD!

MAYBE THIS TIME HE'LL STRIKE OUT..

NO, HE ALWAYS HITS A HOME RUN..I'VE WATCHED IT TWENTY TIMES..IT'S MY FAVORITE SCENE..

HELLO? YES, HE'S HERE..

IT'S FOR YOU..

www.snoopy.com

WATCHING TV..ROY HOBBS IS UP..IT'S MY FAVORITE SCENE...SURE..UH HUH... YES..SURE..UH HUH...

YOU MISSED IT..YOU WERE RIGHT, THOUGH..HE HIT A HOME RUN UP INTO THE LIGHTS..SPARKS FLEW ALL OVER THE FIELD..

5-17

I'M FEEDING YOU EARLY BECAUSE I'M GOING TO A DANCE TONIGHT..

I'M HOPING I GET TO DANCE WITH THE LITTLE RED-HAIRED GIRL, AND...

..AND I DIDN'T KNOW YOU WERE GOING ALONG..

HOLD IT RIGHT THERE, DUDE! THIS IS A DANCE! THE DOG CAN'T COME IN!

THERE WAS A MISUNDERSTANDING.. THIS LITTLE KID THOUGHT IT WAS GOING TO BE A COSTUME BALL SO HE WORE A DOG SUIT..

OKAY, GO ON IN... HAVE A GREAT TIME..

PRETTY GOOD DOG SUIT..

HI, CHARLIE BROWN! WELCOME TO THE DANCE! EVERYONE IS HERE..

I HOPE WE'RE NOT LATE..

THIS ISN'T A COSTUME BALL, IS IT?

NO

THEN WHO'S THE LITTLE KID IN THE DOG SUIT?

63

Panel 1: SEE? THERE SHE IS, CHARLIE BROWN..

Panel 2: THERE'S THE LITTLE RED-HAIRED GIRL JUST WAITING FOR YOU TO ASK HER TO DANCE...

Panel 3: I WISH I WERE SOPHISTICATED LIKE GUYS YOU READ ABOUT IN STORIES..

5-21

Panel 4: HERE'S THE SCOTT FITZGERALD HERO STANDING BY THE PUNCH BOWL "TRYING TO LOOK CASUAL AND UNINTERESTED IN THE DANCERS"

Panel 5: "DON'T GIVE IT ANOTHER THOUGHT, OLD SPORT"

Panel 6: I CAN'T BELIEVE I'M DOING THIS..

5-22

Panel 7: I'M WALKING TOWARD THE LITTLE RED-HAIRED GIRL..

Panel 8: I'M GOING TO ASK HER TO DANCE..I'M GETTING CLOSER.. I'M ALMOST THERE.. I'M ...

Panel 9: CHUCK! WE'VE BEEN LOOKING FOR YOU!

COME ON, CHARLES, THEY'RE PLAYING THE "HOKEY-POKEY"

OH, GOOD GRIEF!

Panel 10: HERE'S GATSBY STANDING BY THE PUNCH BOWL WATCHING COUPLES DANCE BY...

5-23

Panel 11: "IT WAS IN NINETEEN-NINETEEN.. I ONLY STAYED FIVE MONTHS.. THAT'S WHY I CAN'T REALLY CALL MYSELF AN OXFORD MAN"

Panel 12: "BOTH OF US LOVED EACH OTHER ALL THAT TIME, OLD SPORT"

64

CHARLIE BROWN! WHERE HAVE YOU BEEN?

I'VE BEEN DOING THE HOKEY-POKEY WITH PATTY AND MARCIE..

LISTEN..THEY'RE PLAYING A FOX TROT..

NOW I CAN ASK THE LITTLE RED HAIRED GIRL TO DANCE..

I THINK SOMEONE IS AHEAD OF YOU..

5-25

"DAISY AND GATSBY DANCED.. I REMEMBER HIS GRACEFUL CONSERVATIVE FOX TROT"

HEY, KID! AREN'T YOU THE ONE WHOSE FRIEND IS WEARING THE DOG SUIT?

ANYWAY, HE'S SICK.. I THINK HE DRANK TOO MUCH PUNCH..

THE NURSE IS WITH HIM...

SHE'S HAVING TROUBLE GETTING THE DOG SUIT OFF..

5-26

SURE, THERE I WAS HAVING A GOOD TIME AT THE DANCE, AND THEN YOU HAD TO GET SICK..

SOMEONE SAID YOU PROBABLY DRANK TOO MUCH PUNCH..

5-27

I ATE TOO MUCH.. I DRANK TOO MUCH.. AND I DANCED TOO MUCH...

LET'S DO IT AGAIN TOMORROW NIGHT..

THE HOKEY-POKEY WASN'T VERY ROMANTIC, CHUCK

I SAVED YOU THE WALTZ, CHARLES, BUT I NEVER SAW YOU..

HOW ABOUT THE LIMO, CHUCK? WE NEVER SAW A LIMO, EITHER..

HOW COME YOU FELL DOWN DOING THE HOKEY-POKEY?

5-28

DON'T INVITE US TO ANYMORE DANCES, CHUCK

"MANY A HEART IS BROKEN AFTER THE BALL"

GUESS WHAT I LEARNED IN SCHOOL TODAY..

WE WERE HAVING LUNCH, AND I LEARNED HOW TO OPEN A BAG OF POTATO CHIPS..

WHAT'S THE CAPITAL OF NORWAY?

WHO KNOWS?

5-29

DID YOU KNOW THAT GRAMMA AND GRAMPA HAVE MOVED?

MOVED?

GRAMMA SAYS SHE TAKES FOUR PILLS A DAY, THEIR DOGS TAKE EIGHT PILLS A DAY, AND GRAMPA TAKES FIVE PILLS A DAY...

5-30

GRAMMA SAYS THEY'RE LIVING IN PILL CITY..

67

PEANUTS. by SCHULZ

5-31

JUNE 6, 1944 -TO REMEMBER-

YOU KNOW WHAT I AM, CHARLES? I'M A "REMINDER"

WE HAVE A BOOK REPORT DUE TOMORROW..

I KNOW! I KNOW! STOP BUGGING ME!

NOBODY LIKES A "REMINDER"

I'M DOOMED, MARCIE.. I'M GOING TO GET A BAD GRADE IN EVERY SUBJECT..

YOU HAD GOOD ATTENDANCE THOUGH, SIR...

AND YOU DIDN'T SPILL ANYTHING! THAT'S WHAT IT'LL SAY ON YOUR REPORT CARD...

"SHE CAME EVERY DAY, AND SHE DIDN'T SPILL ANYTHING!"

YOU ARE DISPROPORTIONATELY WEIRD, MARCIE..

RATS! I DIDN'T MAKE THE HONOR ROLL!

IF YOU HAVE MOUSIE-BLAH HAIR, YOU NEVER MAKE THE HONOR ROLL..

FOR EIGHT GENERATIONS NO ONE IN OUR FAMILY HAS EVER MADE THE HONOR ROLL..

THEY ALL HAD MOUSIE-BLAH HAIR..

6-4

6-5

LAP LAP LAP
LAP LAP LAP

WHAT COULD I DO? I NEEDED A DRINK OF WATER..

6-6

I DON'T HAVE A DOG NOW, BUT I KNOW I'LL HAVE ONE SOMEDAY...

I WAS WONDERING IF YOU COULD GIVE ME SOME TIPS ON HOW TO TRAIN A DOG...

6-11

YOU DON'T GIVE TIPS?

"RED AT NIGHT.. SAILORS' DELIGHT"

6-12

"RED IN THE MORNING, SAILORS TAKE WARNING"

MAYBE IT'S JUST A LITTLE SQUALL..

TELL YOUR DOG I FOUND A NEW STICK.. TELL HIM I'LL THROW IT, AND HE CAN CHASE IT...

6-13

ARE YOU TELLING HIM?

73

Panel 1: WHAT A FACE! I'LL NEVER BE BEAUTIFUL.. | YOU WILL SOMEDAY, SIR.. ALL OF YOUR FEATURES WILL SETTLE INTO THEIR PROPER SIZES AND PLACES, AND YOU'LL BE BEAUTIFUL

Panel 2: WHAT ABOUT MY HANDS? | SOMEDAY YOU'LL HAVE PRETTY HANDS, SIR..

Panel 3: WHAT ABOUT A CERTAIN FRIEND OF MINE? | SHE'LL BE GORGEOUS!

Panel: WHY ARE YOU SO CRABBY?

Panel: DOG FOOD? WELL, IT USUALLY HAS A HEARTY FLAVOR.. A LITTLE SPICY.. MAYBE A TOUCH OF GAMINESS...

Panel: NO, I DON'T WANT TO KNOW WHAT A WORM TASTES LIKE..

79

HERE'S A GREAT CAMP WE CAN GO TO, MARCIE..

I'M NOT GOING TO CAMP THIS YEAR..I'M GOING TO STAY HOME AND TAKE VIOLIN LESSONS..

YOU'RE GOING TO **WHAT**?

I'VE ALWAYS WANTED TO PLAY THE VIOLIN..

YOU'D GIVE UP SWIMMING, RIDING, ARCHERY AND CANOEING FOR PLAYING THE VIOLIN?

YOU CAN'T PLAY BRAHMS ON A CANOE PADDLE, SIR..

© 1998 United Feature Syndicate, Inc.

www.snoopy.com

CHECK THIS OUT, CHUCK..GREAT LOOKING CAMP, HUH?

I'M NOT SURE I'M GOING TO CAMP THIS YEAR..

6-28

OH, SURE! CAN'T PLAY BRAHMS ON A CANOE PADDLE, HUH?

I NEVER KNOW WHAT ANYONE'S TALKING ABOUT..

HI, CHUCK..JUST THOUGHT I'D CALL AGAIN..

WOOF

7-2

WHAT? NO, JUST CURIOUS AS TO HOW YOU'VE BEEN..

WOOF WOOF WOOF

YOU'RE STARTING TO REPEAT YOURSELF, CHUCK..

© 1998 United Feature Syndicate, Inc.

CHARLES, PATTY THINKS YOU DON'T CALL HER BECAUSE SHE ISN'T CUTE..

7-3

BECAUSE SHE HAS FRECKLES AND A BIG NOSE

BECAUSE SHE HAS FRECKLES AND A BIG NOSE

SO IS THAT WHY YOU DON'T CALL HER?

SO IS THAT WHY YOU DON'T CALL HER?

THIS ISN'T WORKING, IS IT?

HE SAID HE WAS MISSING HIS FAVORITE PROGRAM..

© 1998 United Feature Syndicate, Inc.

MY GRAMMA USED TO READ DOG DISHES..

7-4

AFTER WE WERE THROUGH EATING, SHE'D TAKE A DOG DISH, LOOK AT IT CAREFULLY, AND TELL US THE FUTURE..

GRAMMA SAID DOG DISHES WERE MORE ACCURATE THAN TEA LEAVES..

© 1998 United Feature Syndicate, Inc.

REALLY? I NEVER HEARD OF A GRAMMA WHO READ WORMS..

82

7-6

I KNEW IT! YOUR EARS ARE STILL JUMPING!

He began to feel uncomfortable with others in the family.

He knew it was important for those who share a home to have similar moral values.

So the dog left.

7-7

7-8

GOTTA SAVE THE OL' THROWIN' ARM, MANAGER..

THE GAME'S BEEN CALLED, CHARLIE BROWN..

BUT IT'S CLEARING UP! I CAN SEE BLUE SKY!

THAT ISN'T BLUE SKY..THOSE ARE LIGHTS FROM THE MALL..

IT LOOKS LIKE BLUE SKY TO ME..I KNOW IT'S BLUE SKY..IT'S CLEARING UP..I CAN SEE BLUE SKY..

ANYONE GOING TO THE MALL?

I JUST SAW A FARMER BEING INTERVIEWED ON TV.. HE SAID HE WAS GLAD TO SEE A LITTLE RAIN..

WAS HIS TEAM LEADING BY TEN RUNS WHEN THE GAME WAS CALLED?

I DON'T THINK THEY SAID ANYTHING ABOUT A BASEBALL GAME..

I'LL GO BACK AND WATCH SOME MORE.. I'LL LET YOU KNOW WHAT THEY SAY..

I HOPE HIS TRACTOR GETS WET!

I'LL NEVER FORGET THE EXPRESSION ON THE OTHER ATTORNEY'S FACE...

HE SAW I HAD THIS BRAND-NEW YELLOW LEGAL PAD WITH LINES ON IT..

THERE'S A LOT OF JEALOUSY AMONG ATTORNEYS

85

PEANUTS by Schulz

HEY, MANAGER..

ASK YOUR CATCHER IF HE WANTS TO GO OVER TO MY HOUSE AFTER THE GAME FOR SOME LEMONADE..

SHE WANTS TO KNOW IF YOU WANT TO GO OVER TO HER HOUSE AFTER THE GAME FOR SOME LEMONADE..

TELL HER I WOULDN'T GO OVER TO HER HOUSE IF THEY WERE GIVING AWAY SPORTS CARS, THOUSAND DOLLAR BILLS, AND CHOCOLATE SUNDAES!

HE SAYS...

© 1998 United Feature Syndicate, Inc.

www.snoopy.com

YOU WOULDN'T?

7-12

MY ARM HURTS..

WHY DON'T YOU LET ME PITCH? I HAVE A CUTE ARM!

PITCHERS DON'T HAVE CUTE ARMS!

I'LL BET TY COBB HAD A CUTE ARM, DIDN'T SHE?

DO DOGS EVER LOOK AT CLOUDS?

IF I COULD TALK, I'D TELL YOU HOW WE LOOK AT CLOUDS, AND BIRDS, AND THE MOON AND EVERYTHING, BUT DOGS CAN'T TALK..

I GUESS DOGS NEVER LOOK AT CLOUDS..

STUPID KID!

MY EYES KIND OF HURT.. I THINK I'VE BEEN WATCHING TOO MUCH TUMBLEWEED..

7-20

SEE? THAT MEANS AN HOUR HAS GONE BY..

7-21

LET'S TURN IT OVER, AND WATCH IT AGAIN..

WOW! LOOK AT THAT! OKAY, NOW WE'LL TURN IT OVER AND WATCH IT AGAIN..

I LEAD A DUMB LIFE!

A GOOD MANAGER KNOWS HOW TO COMMUNICATE WITH HIS PLAYERS..

7-22

A GOOD MANAGER EVEN SHOWS CONCERN FOR THEIR WELFARE..

HOW'VE YOU BEEN?

91

HERE'S THE WORLD WAR I FLYING ACE CROSSING NO MAN'S LAND TO VISIT HIS BROTHER SPIKE..

HI, SPIKE..HOW ARE THINGS IN THE TRENCHES?

NOT QUITE WHAT I EXPECTED..

THE FIRST THING I NOTICED WHEN I GOT HERE IS THERE AREN'T ANY DRINKING FOUNTAINS..

ANOTHER ROOT BEER FOR MY BROTHER SPIKE, S'IL VOUS PLAÎT..

I HAD A GIRL FRIEND BACK HOME, BUT SHE'S STOPPED WRITING TO ME..

HERE'S TO ALL THE GIRL FRIENDS WHO DON'T WRITE TO US ANYMORE..

RATS!

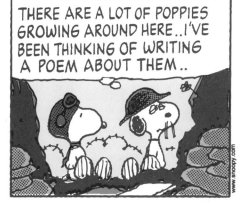

THERE ARE A LOT OF POPPIES GROWING AROUND HERE..I'VE BEEN THINKING OF WRITING A POEM ABOUT THEM..

"IN SUCH AND SUCH FIELDS THE POPPIES BLOW.."

I CAN'T FINISH IT BECAUSE I DON'T KNOW WHERE WE ARE..

96

MOM SHOULD LET US HAVE A DOG..

CLOMP!

8-9

© 1998 United Feature Syndicate, Inc.

www.snoopy.com

HAVING A DOG COULD BE FUN, DON'T YOU THINK?

I DECIDED TO WRITE A LETTER..

GOOD FOR YOU..

HOW DO YOU SPELL "BY THE WAY"?

JUST THE WAY IT SOUNDS.. "BY THE WAY"

Dear Grandma,
How have you been? By the way, thanks for the Christmas present.

YOU DID IT AGAIN! YOU TOOK MY COMIC BOOKS WITHOUT ASKING ME!

THESE ARE **MY** COMIC BOOKS, AND I DON'T WANT YOU TOUCHING THEM!

IF YOU DO IT AGAIN, I'M GOING TO HIT YOU RIGHT OVER THE HEAD!

I'M GLAD WE HAD THIS DISCUSSION..

THE FIRST THING YOU DO IS RAISE YOUR GLASS..

THEN YOU SAY, "I'LL DRINK TO THAT!"

IT TAKES A LITTLE PRACTICE..

 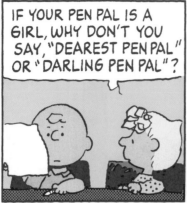  

 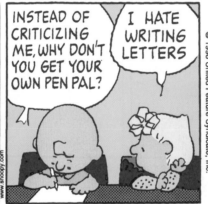 

100

WAS I CUTE WHEN I WAS A BABY?

NOT AT ALL

ACTUALLY, YOU WERE UN-CUTE..

HOW UN-CUTE?

I SUPPOSE YOU REALIZE THAT SCHOOL STARTS AGAIN NEXT MONTH..

I'M READY, KID..

I COME FROM A FAMILY OF DEDICATED SCHOOL BUILDINGS..

WE'RE A PROUD FAMILY...

OUR OLDER SISTER HAS A NEW CAFETERIA..

103

HELLO, CHUCK?

MY BROTHER ISN'T HERE.. HE JUST LEFT FOR CAMP..

CAMP? I THOUGHT HE WASN'T GOING THIS YEAR..

8-24

I DON'T KNOW.. MAYBE HE CHANGED HIS MIND..

ANYWAY, I CAN'T TALK NOW..I'M MOVING MY THINGS INTO HIS ROOM..

© 1998 United Feature Syndicate, Inc.

WHAT'S GOING ON HERE?

BIG BROTHER! I THOUGHT YOU WENT TO CAMP..

I ONLY WENT OVER TO THE MALL..I'M GONE FOR THIRTY MINUTES, AND YOU START MOVING YOUR STUFF INTO MY ROOM?!

THAT'S MY NEW PHILOSOPHY.."IF YOU SEE A ROOM YOU LIKE, MOVE INTO IT.."

8-25

© 1998 United Feature Syndicate, Inc.

I'M GOING INTO THE KITCHEN TO HAVE BREAKFAST..I'LL ONLY BE IN THERE FOR MAYBE FIFTEEN MINUTES...

WHILE I'M GONE, PLEASE DON'T START MOVING YOUR THINGS INTO MY ROOM..

8-26

© 1998 United Feature Syndicate, Inc.

I'LL PUT THESE SWEATERS BACK..

PEANUTS by Schulz

PSYCHIATRIC HELP 5¢

THE DOCTOR IS IN OUT AND ABOUT

WHAT WE'RE TALKING ABOUT HERE, CHARLIE BROWN, IS COMMUNICATION

THE DOCTOR IS IN

I DON'T NECESSARILY MEAN WORDS..SOMETIMES BODY LANGUAGE TELLS US EVEN MORE..

BODY LANGUAGE?

THAT'S INTERESTING..BODY LANGUAGE..COMMUNICATION..

THE DOCTOR IS IN

MY RIGHT FIELDER IS REALLY STUPID..I TRY TO EXPLAIN THINGS TO HER, BUT I DON'T GET ANYPLACE..

MAYBE IT'S COMMUNICATION.. WHAT DO YOU THINK?

HELP 5¢

8-30

THE DOCTOR IS IN

PSYCHIATRISTS ARE BIG ON BODY LANGUAGE..

107

HEY, MARCIE..HOW SOON BEFORE SCHOOL STARTS AGAIN?

I MAY HAVE TO BORROW SOME NOTEBOOK PAPER AND THINGS..

SO HOW SOON BEFORE SCHOOL STARTS?

DO YOU HAVE A CALENDAR?

A WHAT?

THIS IS WHAT WE CAME FOR, TROOPS.. LOOK AT THAT VIEW!

HEY, MANAGER.. NEXT YEAR I THINK I'LL PLAY FOR A DIFFERENT TEAM..

I'M TIRED OF LOSING ALL THE TIME..

I SUPPOSE YOU'RE GOING TO PLAY FOR SOMEONE ELSE, TOO..

I PLAY FOR WHOEVER OWNS THE SUPPER DISH

HOW SHOULD I CHEER FOR YOUR TEAM TODAY, CHARLES?

SHOULD I YELL, "GO, REDS!" OR "GO, BLUES!" OR "GO, GREENS!" OR WHAT?

I DON'T KNOW, RERUN..YELL ANYTHING YOU WANT..

GO, T-SHIRTS!

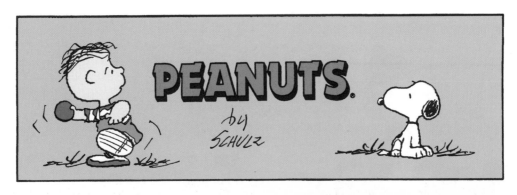

THAT LOOKS LIKE A GOOD GAME..

WHAT DO YOU CALL IT?

SLOBBER BALL..

HAS THE SCHOOL BUS COME YET?

IF IT HAD, DO YOU THINK I'D STILL BE STANDING HERE?

9-10

© 1998 United Feature Syndicate, Inc.

BOO!

WHAT ARE THOSE ROUND THINGS?

PEOPLE FACES..

9-11

I'M DRAWING A FOOTBALL STADIUM FILLED WITH SIXTY-THOUSAND FANS..

© 1998 United Feature Syndicate, Inc.

I ONLY SEE TEN..

PARKING WAS A PROBLEM..

WHEN I WAS LITTLE, THE SCHOOL BUS CAME BY WHERE WE LIVED..

9-12

I USED TO JUMP UP AND DOWN AND BARK, AND ALL THE KIDS WOULD YELL AND WAVE..

© 1998 United Feature Syndicate, Inc.

DID YOU USED TO WAVE WHEN THE CACTUS BUS WENT BY?

YES, MA'AM, I BROUGHT MY DOG TO SCHOOL BECAUSE HE WAS FEELING LONELY..

9-14

YES, MA'AM..HE'S KIND OF SMART..

TELL HER I CAN SPELL "ZAMBONI"

© 1998 United Feature Syndicate, Inc.

9-15

KICK THE BALL, MARCIE! WHAT ARE YOU WAITING FOR? WHAT ARE YOU LOOKING AT?

IT DOESN'T SAY, "LOW FAT"

© 1998 United Feature Syndicate, Inc.

PSST, FRANKLIN.. WHAT'D YOU PUT DOWN FOR NUMBER SIX?

I PUT DOWN "EIGHT"

"EIGHT"? EIGHT WHAT?

"EIGHT" NOTHING.. JUST "EIGHT"

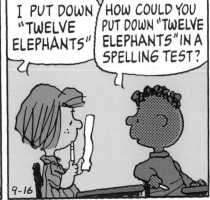I PUT DOWN "TWELVE ELEPHANTS"

HOW COULD YOU PUT DOWN "TWELVE ELEPHANTS" IN A SPELLING TEST?

9-16

© 1998 United Feature Syndicate, Inc.

WHAT ROOM ARE WE IN?

YES, MA'AM..I'M SURE SHE'S ASLEEP..

SHOULD I WAKE HER UP?

I THINK IT'S TIME FOR HER TEN O'CLOCK FEEDING..

I'M AWAKE!

PRINCIPAL'S OFFICE

YES, YOUR HONOR, MY CLIENT WAS STANDING ALONE IN THE FIELD MINDING HIS OWN BUSINESS..

SUDDENLY, WITHOUT WARNING, HE WAS ATTACKED BY THREE OF THE FARMER'S CROWS!

HE SAYS TO STOP SCATTERING STRAW ON THE FLOOR..

YES, MA'AM.. I'M READY

I HAVE MY REPORT RIGHT HERE... WELL, NOT EXACTLY RIGHT HERE..

ACTUALLY, MY SECRETARY STILL HAS IT.. SHE TYPED IT FOR ME LAST NIGHT..

9-20

WAS THAT YOU SIGHING, MA'AM?

HEY, CHUCK, YOU READY FOR SOME BACK YARD FOOTBALL?

9-21

ME AN' MARCIE CAN GET OVER THERE ANYTIME YOU'RE READY..

I THINK WE'VE MOVED AWAY, AND I DON'T KNOW WHAT OUR NEW ADDRESS IS..

© 1998 United Feature Syndicate, Inc.

OKAY, MARCIE, GO STRAIGHT OUT AND CUT RIGHT..

I CUT LEFT BETTER, SIR..

9-22

IF YOU CUT LEFT, THE BALL WON'T BE THERE..

© 1998 United Feature Syndicate, Inc.

THAT'S NOT A BAD IDEA..

THAT WAS A GOOD PRACTICE, HUH, MARCIE?

NO! I THINK I BROKE ALL MY ARMS AND THIRTY FINGERS..

WELL, WE'RE GETTING YOU TOUGHENED UP FOR THE NEW SEASON, HUH?

© 1998 United Feature Syndicate, Inc.

I'M NOT INTERESTED IN GETTING TOUGHENED UP..

I'LL NEVER UNDERSTAND YOU, MARCIE..

9-23

COME ON.. YOU'VE GOT TO SEE THIS..

THE MOON IS BRIGHT, AND THERE'S A CHILL IN THE AIR..

THIS WAY..STAY CLOSE BEHIND ME..

KIND OF SPOOKY, ISN'T IT?

SEE? THIS IS THE TIME OF NIGHT THE ZAMBONIS COME OUT..

WHAT I THINK I'LL DO IS GO INTO TOWN, AND STAND SOMEPLACE, LIKE MAYBE ON A CORNER..

9-28

THEN A BEAUTIFUL HOLLYWOOD-TYPE GIRL WILL COME BY IN A CONVERTIBLE AND TAKE ME TO HER HOME..

I'LL HAVE TO MAKE SURE I LOOK SOPHISTICATED..

© 1998 United Feature Syndicate, Inc.

I'LL WEAR MY MICKEY MOUSE SHOES

HEY, MA! SEE THE FUNNY LOOKING DOG!

WHAT'S HE STANDING HERE FOR? ISN'T HE FUNNY LOOKING?

9-29

DID YOU SEE THE FUNNY HAT HE WAS WEARING AND THE FUNNY LOOKING SHOES?

© 1998 United Feature Syndicate, Inc.

MICKEY MOUSE SHOES ARE NOT FUNNY LOOKING!

SOMETIMES IF YOU STAND NEAR THE CORNER, A BEAUTIFUL HOLLYWOOD-TYPE GIRL WILL COME BY IN A CONVERTIBLE, AND TAKE YOU HOME..

"ANIMAL CLINIC"?

WHY AM I STANDING IN FRONT OF AN "ANIMAL CLINIC"?

9-30

© 1998 United Feature Syndicate, Inc.

THE DOCTOR WILL SEE YOU NOW!

WE SAW YOU STANDING IN FRONT OF OUR "ANIMAL CLINIC".. MOM IS THE VET HERE.. SHE SAID, "THAT DOG DOESN'T LOOK WELL.. BRING HIM IN HERE.."

IT'S TOO BAD DOGS CAN'T TALK.. IF YOU COULD TALK, YOU COULD TELL ME HOW YOU FEEL, AND WHAT YOU'RE THINKING..

DID ANYBODY TAKE MY MICKEY MOUSE SHOES?

10-5

10-6

MOM SAYS YOU NEED EXERCISE..

SHE SAID I SHOULD WALK WITH YOU UP AND DOWN THE HALL AT LEAST TWICE A DAY..

I CAN'T STEER THIS THING!

HERE, SPIKE.. I BROUGHT YOU SOME TAPIOCA..

MOM SAYS YOU HAD DISTEMPER, BUT YOU'RE GETTING BETTER..

MAYBE YOU'LL BE ABLE TO GO HOME SOON..

DON'T CURE ME.. THIS IS A GOOD LIFE..

10-7

123

 GUESS WHAT, SPIKE.. MOM SAYS YOU CAN GO HOME TODAY..

I HAVE TO CARRY YOU BECAUSE SHE SAID YOU'RE TOO WEAK TO WALK

THIS IS WHERE YOU LIVE?

LIVE?

10-8

 MY PLAN WAS TO GET ADOPTED BY SOME BEAUTIFUL GIRL, BUT INSTEAD I ENDED UP IN THE HOSPITAL..

ANYWAY, HERE I AM BACK HOME AGAIN.. I GUESS I'M REALLY PRETTY LUCKY..

10-9

I STILL HAVE MY MICKEY MOUSE SHOES AND A FAITHFUL FRIEND TO LEAN ON..

OUCH!

MOM, A COUPLE OF DOGS JUST WALKED BY..THEY ALMOST LOOKED LIKE THEY COULD BE SPIKE'S BROTHERS..

NO, THEY SEEMED TO BE GOING SOMEPLACE

I WONDER WHY THAT GIRL WAS LOOKING AT US..

PROBABLY ADMIRING US..

10-10

LET'S SAY WE'RE MARRIED, AND MY DAD HAS OFFERED YOU A MILLION DOLLAR A YEAR JOB WITH HIS COMPANY..

10-15

BUT LET'S SAY YOU INSIST ON PLAYING YOUR STUPID PIANO IN SOME SLEAZY JOINT, AND...

KLUNK!

I NEVER GET TO THE PART ABOUT THE LIMO AND THE FREE LUNCHES..

WHEN YOU'RE ALONE IN THE DESERT, YOU SING SONGS ABOUT LONELINESS..

10-16

YOU SING ABOUT LOVE, AND THE MOON, AND THE STARS AND THE ALAMO..

MAYBE YOU COULD LIP-SYNC..

SEE? SHE SAYS YOU TAKE THE BOWL OUT OF THE CUPBOARD, POUR THE CEREAL INTO THE BOWL, AND THEN ADD THE MILK..

THIS IS YOUR "BASIC COOKING" PROGRAM..

10-17

127

PEANUTS by SCHULZ

THIS IS MY REPORT ON THE FOOTBALL CAREER OF MOSES..

YES, MA'AM.. THAT MOSES... YOU DIDN'T?

© 1998 United Feature Syndicate, Inc.

ANYWAY, WHEN MOSES WAS YOUNG, HE SHOWED GREAT PROMISE..ALL THE PROFESSIONAL TEAMS WANTED HIM..

YES, MA'AM.. FOOTBALL TEAMS..

WELL, WE ALL KNOW HOW HE WENT UP ON THE MOUNTAIN, AND THEN CARRIED THOSE TABLETS OF STONE BACK DOWN..

THIS PROBABLY WAS HOW HE HURT HIS THROWING ARM..AFTER THAT, HE COULD NEVER THROW THE LONG BALL..

www.snoopy.com

HE COULD ONLY THROW A FEW SHORT SIDELINE PATTERNS..

10-18

PRETTY SOON HE GOT INVOLVED IN OTHER THINGS AND QUIT FOOTBALL..

RESEARCH? NO, MA'AM..MY GRAMPA..WELL, I FIGURE HE MUST HAVE KNOWN HIM..

I GUESS GRAMPA ISN'T AS OLD AS I THOUGHT HE WAS..

LET'S COMPARE NOTES, SIR, AND SEE IF WE'VE GOT THE SAME ANSWERS..

"TRUE, FALSE, MAYBE, WHO KNOWS? WHY NOT? SURE, WHEN? THEY DID? SOMETIME, I DID NOT, WHO, ME? IT WAS DARK, AND EVERYONE WAS GETTING HUNGRY"

I DON'T KNOW HOW YOU DO IT, SIR..

NEVER LET 'EM KNOW WHERE YOU'RE COMING FROM, MARCIE..

GOOD MORNING..I'M HERE TO ASK IF YOU'D CARE TO SUBSCRIBE TO THE "GREAT PUMPKIN" NEWSLETTER

GET OFF OUR PORCH OR I'LL SIC OUR DOG ON YOU!

I'M SORRY.. I DIDN'T MEAN TO BOTHER YOU..

THAT'S ALL RIGHT.. WE DON'T HAVE A DOG..

HERE, WE'RE GIVING AWAY A DOUGHNUT WITH EVERY SUBSCRIPTION TO THE "GREAT PUMPKIN" NEWSLETTER

I'LL TAKE A DOUGHNUT, BUT I WOULDN'T READ YOUR NEWSLETTER IF IT WERE THE LAST NEWSLETTER ON EARTH..

TAKE ONE WITH COCONUT ON IT..

GOOD MORNING.. WOULD YOU BE INTERESTED IN SUBSCRIBING TO OUR "GREAT PUMPKIN" NEWSLETTER?

DOES IT HAVE CARTOONS IN IT?

YOU SHOULD GET SOMEONE TO DRAW CARTOONS IN IT..

WHAT'S THE NAME OF THE GUY WHO DRAWS "DILBERT"?

GOOD MORNING.. I'M HERE TO TELL YOU ABOUT THE "GREAT PUMPKIN".

HEY, MA! THERE'S A FALSE PROPHET AT THE DOOR.. WHAT SHOULD I TELL HIM?

REALLY?

HE'S GONE.. I THINK HE HEARD YOU, MA..

WE'LL RUN THIS PICTURE IN THE NEXT "GREAT PUMPKIN" NEWSLETTER..

READERS WILL SEE DEDICATED BELIEVERS SITTING IN A PUMPKIN PATCH WAITING FOR THE "GREAT PUMPKIN"

IF WE'RE LUCKY, NO ONE WILL RECOGNIZE US..

IF ANYBODY ASKS, MY NAME IS "REX"

130

SNOOPY, IT MAKES ME FEEL GOOD TO KNOW THAT I CAN ALWAYS TALK TO YOU ABOUT THE "GREAT PUMPKIN."

OF COURSE, IT JUST MIGHT BE THAT IT'S BECAUSE DOGS BELIEVE EVERYTHING YOU TELL THEM..

MOST DOGS..

10-26

AND MY BROTHER TALKS ALL THE TIME ABOUT THIS "GREAT PUMPKIN" THING, SEE..

SO SOMETIMES I THINK HE'S REALLY CRAZY, AND..

10-27

AND THEN I WONDER ABOUT THE REST OF OUR FAMILY, AND...

SO WE'LL GO FROM HOUSE TO HOUSE "TRICK OR TREATING," AND PEOPLE WILL GIVE US THINGS..

LIKE MAYBE A BICYCLE?

NO, NOT A BICYCLE.. MAYBE AN ORANGE OR A COOKIE..

A BICYCLE WOULD BE NICE..

YOU HAVE TO TAKE WHATEVER THEY GIVE YOU..

HOW DID I GET INVOLVED IN SOMETHING LIKE THIS?

10-28

132

HERE'S THE BAG YOU'LL USE TO CARRY ALL THE THINGS PEOPLE WILL GIVE YOU WHEN WE GO "TRICK OR TREATING" ON HALLOWEEN NIGHT

WHAT IF SOMEBODY GIVES ME A BICYCLE?

NOBODY'S GOING TO GIVE YOU A BICYCLE..

I'LL JUST SAY, "THANK YOU..DON'T PUT IT IN THE BAG..I'LL RIDE IT HOME!"

HEY! AREN'T YOU GOING TO SIT IN THE PUMPKIN PATCH, AND WAIT FOR THE "GREAT PUMPKIN"?

WE'RE NOT AS STUPID AS YOU..WE'RE GOING "TRICK OR TREATING"

MAYBE I'LL JUST SAY, SORT OF JOKINGLY, "THANK YOU, JUST PUT THE BICYCLE IN THIS BAG"

I CAN'T STAND IT..

FOR "TRICK OR TREATS" I GOT TWELVE CANDY BARS, FOURTEEN COOKIES, AND THREE TUBES OF TOOTHPASTE

I DIDN'T GET A BICYCLE..

I LOVE THE FEEL OF NEW BOOKS, MARCIE.. THE PRETTY COVERS, THE PRINT, EVEN THE SMELL..

DO YOU EVER READ ANY OF THEM?

DO I EVER WHAT?

I DON'T KNOW..HOW CAN YOU GET YOUR FOOT CAUGHT IN A NEST?

135

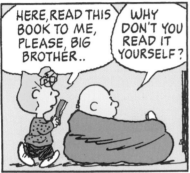

HERE, READ THIS BOOK TO ME, PLEASE, BIG BROTHER..

WHY DON'T YOU READ IT YOURSELF?

I HATE READING..

JUST READ THE EXCITING PARTS..SKIP THE BORING PARTS AND DESCRIPTIONS..

"HIS NAME WAS DOUGLAS, AND ONE DAY HE..."

WHAT DO YOU MEAN, "HE"? READ SOMETHING ABOUT A "SHE.."

THEY SAY THE FAMILY THAT READS TOGETHER STAYS TOGETHER

WHERE DID YOU HEAR THAT?

I READ IT..

MAYBE SOMEBODY READ IT TO ME..

YES, MA'AM.. REQUEST PERMISSION TO GO SEE THE SCHOOL NURSE..

I FEEL AN ANXIETY ATTACK COMING ON..

HURRY, SIR! SHE'S GOING TO GET THERE BEFORE YOU DO!

SO YOU'RE GOING TO FLY SOUTH FOR THE WINTER..

I SUPPOSE YOU REALIZE IT'S A LONG WAY..

// /\ /\?

NO, I DON'T WANT TO CARRY YOU..

IF YOU'RE GOING TO FLY SOUTH, I SUGGEST YOU'D BETTER GET STARTED..

YES, TODAY IS SATURDAY..WHAT'S WRONG WITH TRAVELING ON SATURDAY?

WORMS ARE CLOSED ON THE WEEKEND?

140

141

PEANUTS.

by SCHULZ

HERE'S THE WORLD FAMOUS PATRIOT SOLDIER AT. VALLEY **FORGE**

ALL RIGHT, I SAID I'D TELL HIM, AND I WILL..

11-22

I STILL DON'T THINK HE'LL LISTEN TO ME..

YES, SIR..I'D LIKE **PERMISSION** TO SEE GENERAL WASHINGTON..

WELL, YES, I'D SAY IT CAUSES SUFFERING..

© 1998 United Feature Syndicate, Inc.

YES, GENERAL ... I UNDERSTAND..

www.snoopy.com

I KNEW HE HAD OTHER THINGS ON HIS MIND..

WHAT I SAID WAS, "SIR, WE KEEP LOSING THESE WHITE PING PONG BALLS IN THE SNOW"

SCHULZ

I'M STARTING MY OWN POLLING FIRM.. SEE? I WROTE DOWN WHAT I THINK ABOUT EVERYTHING..

ARE YOU GOING TO GO FROM HOUSE TO HOUSE, AND ASK OTHER PEOPLE WHAT THEY THINK?

WHO CARES WHAT OTHER PEOPLE THINK?

"DETAILS AT ELEVEN!" THAT'S MY NEW PHILOSOPHY..

ASK ME WHAT I DID TODAY..

WHAT DID YOU DO TODAY?

DETAILS AT ELEVEN!

"...IN HOPES THAT ST. NICHOLAS SOON WOULD BE THERE"

THAT'S MY FAVORITE POEM.. YOU SHOULD WRITE SOMETHING LIKE THAT..

"Twas the month before Christmas"

I'M LEANING INTO THE WIND BECAUSE THERE'S A BLIZZARD COMING..

IF YOU'RE LEANING INTO THE WIND, YOUR EARS SHOULD BE BLOWING BACK..

THAT'S BETTER..

CLOSE ALL THE SCHOOLS! CLOSE ALL THE SCHOOLS!

12-1

YES, MA'AM? WELL, I THOUGHT MAYBE A BLIZZARD MIGHT BE HEADED THIS WAY..

YES, MA'AM..GET OUT YOUR BOOTS..CHANGE THE ANTIFREEZE IN YOUR CAR.. CHECK STORED VEGETABLES, AND REMOVE ANY THAT SHOW SIGNS OF ROTTING..

ANYTHING ELSE? YES, MA'AM..

12-2

BRING THE DOG IN..

147

148

149

"OBJECTS IN THE WATER DISH ARE CLOSER THAN THEY APPEAR"

I THOUGHT I'D PUT BOTH OF OUR NAMES ON OUR CHRISTMAS CARDS THIS YEAR..

IS THAT ALL RIGHT WITH YOU? GOOD..

Merry Christmas from Spike and Joe Cactus

WHEN? WHEN DO I EVER GET MY WAY?!

YOU CAN NEVER KNOW IF YOU'RE GOING TO GET YOUR WAY..SOMETIMES YOU DO, AND SOMETIMES YOU DON'T..

I LIKE TO KNOW AHEAD OF TIME..

YES, MA'AM.. ABOUT THIS BOOK..

DO WE HAVE TO READ THE WHOLE BOOK?

I MEAN, DO WE HAVE TO READ THE PREFACE, THE DEDICATION, THE INTRODUCTION AND THE SELECTED BIBLIOGRAPHY?

12-10

NO, WE DON'T MIND READING THE PAGE NUMBERS..

A LITTLE SARCASM THERE, HUH, MA'AM?

"SO WADDYA THINK?" THAT'S MY NEW PHILOSOPHY.. "SO WADDYA THINK?"

ABOUT WHAT?

WHO CARES? SO WADDYA THINK?

12-11

IT'S A DOG'S LIFE, ISN'T IT? SO WADDYA THINK?

I'M NOT SURE.. LET'S TRY IT AGAIN WITHOUT THE RED NOSE..

12-12

151

YES, MA'AM..IT'S REALLY A TWO-EDGED SWORD, ISN'T IT?

IS THE GLASS HALF FULL OR HALF EMPTY? IS IT SIX OF ONE OR HALF A DOZEN OF ANOTHER? IS THIS REALLY FOR THE GREATER PUBLIC GOOD?

12-14

I LIVE FOR YOUR ANSWERS, SIR..

GOOD MORNING..WOULD YOU LIKE TO BUY A HAND-DRAWN PICTURE OF SANTA CLAUS?

12-15

SLAM!

I ASSUME FROM YOUR RESPONSE THAT YOU'RE NOT INTERESTED..

HOW WOULD YOU LIKE TO BUY A HAND-DRAWN PICTURE OF SANTA CLAUS?

THIS DOESN'T LOOK LIKE SANTA CLAUS.. IT LOOKS MORE LIKE "DAFFY DUCK"

12-16

I'LL BET YOU DIDN'T KNOW I CAN DRAW "DAFFY DUCK"!

153

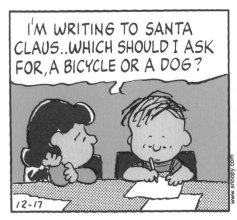

I'M WRITING TO SANTA CLAUS..WHICH SHOULD I ASK FOR, A BICYCLE OR A DOG?

I THINK MAYBE A DOG..

YOU CAN'T FALL OFF A DOG..

SO WHEN SANTA CLAUS BRINGS ME A DOG, I WON'T HAVE TO BORROW YOU ANYMORE..

I'LL THROW THE BALL, AND MY NEW DOG, THAT SANTA CLAUS IS GOING TO BRING ME, WILL CHASE IT..

ANYWAY, I JUST WANT TO THANK YOU FOR ALL THE GOOD TIMES WE'VE HAD...

I'LL PROBABLY CALL MY NEW DOG "ROVER"... I'LL SAY, "HERE, ROVER! GET THE BALL"

LOOK OUT, ROVER

WHEN SANTA CLAUS BRINGS ME THE DOG, WILL HE LEAVE IT ON THE FRONT PORCH OR IN THE BACK YARD? HE WOULDN'T DROP IT DOWN THE CHIMNEY, WOULD HE?

THERE'S SOMETHING I SORT OF FEEL I SHOULD TELL YOU..

MAYBE HE'LL JUST LEAVE A GIFT CERTIFICATE..

PEANUTS by SCHULZ

HELP ME, LINUS.. I WANT TO MAKE A SPECIAL CHRISTMAS CARD FOR THE LITTLE RED-HAIRED GIRL..

DRAW A TREE, CHARLIE BROWN, WITH SOME TINY RED HEARTS HANGING ON IT..

THEN WRITE SOMETHING SORT OF PERSONAL AT THE BOTTOM...

www.snoopy.com

WHAT'S GOING ON? IS MY SWEET BABBOO HELPING MY BIG BROTHER DRAW A CHRISTMAS CARD?

I'M NOT YOUR SWEET BABBOO!!

© 1998 United Feature Syndicate, Inc.

12-20

THAT IS SO STUPID! THAT IS SO HUMONGOUSLY STUPID!

THERE! HOW DOES THAT LOOK? I DREW A TREE WITH LITTLE HEARTS ON IT..

"MERRY CHRISTMAS FROM YOUR SWEET BABBOO"?!

IT'S A FAMILY EXPRESSION..

YES, SIR..MY NAME IS RERUN..DID YOU KNOW THAT SANTA CLAUS IS GOING TO BRING ME A DOG?

SO WHAT I NEED IS A LEASH, AND A COLLAR, AND A SUPPER DISH...

12-21

AND YOU CAN JUST PUT IT ON MY TAB..

© 1998 United Feature Syndicate, Inc.

I NEED YOUR ADVICE, CHARLIE BROWN...

WHEN SANTA CLAUS BRINGS ME MY DOG, I'LL HAVE TO LEARN HOW TO TAKE CARE OF HIM..

12-22

IF YOU SHOW ME WHAT YOU FEED YOUR DOG AND WHERE HE SLEEPS, MAYBE I'LL LEARN SOMETHING..

WHAT'S THAT KID DOING ON THE RUNWAY?

© 1998 United Feature Syndicate, Inc.

LISTEN TO ME..MOM DOESN'T WANT YOU TO HAVE A DOG, DOES SHE?

NO..

DO YOU REALLY THINK SANTA CLAUS IS GOING TO BRING YOU SOMETHING MOM DOESN'T WANT YOU TO HAVE?

OOO!! SUPREME COURT STUFF!

12-23

© 1998 United Feature Syndicate, Inc.

156

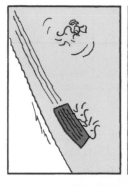

Dear Grandma, Thank you for the money you sent me for Christmas.

I plan to save it for my college education

YOU SPENT IT ALL YESTERDAY..

Everyone says the sweater looks good on me.

12-28

Dear Other Grandma,

"OTHER GRANDMA"?

YESTERDAY I WROTE TO ONE GRANDMA.. TODAY I'M WRITING TO MY OTHER GRANDMA..

HOW CAN YOU TELL WHICH IS WHICH?

12-29

IT DOESN'T MATTER..ALL GRANDMAS LOOK ALIKE FROM A DISTANCE..

HEY, MARCIE..YOU KNOW THE BOOK WE WERE SUPPOSED TO READ? I READ THE WHOLE THING!

WHAT YOU MEAN IS, YOU SAW THE MOVIE ON TV..

12-30

BUT I WROTE A GOOD REPORT..

WHAT YOU MEAN IS, YOU COPIED IT OUT OF THE TV GUIDE..

DON'T ASK ME TO BE A BRIDESMAID AT YOUR WEDDING, MARCIE..I'M BUSY THAT DAY..

THIS? THIS IS A CALENDAR..

IT TELLS YOU WHAT DAY IT IS, WHAT MONTH IT IS, AND WHAT YEAR IT IS..

© 1998 United Feature Syndicate, Inc.

? NO, IT DOESN'T TELL YOU WHERE YOUR MOM IS..

12-31

snoopy.com

* **Download Shockwave movies and PEANUTS cursors.**

* **Read classic PEANUTS comic strips.**

* **Play games including crossword puzzles and a Shockwave baseball game.**

Come visit www.**SNOOPY**.com, the official **PEANUTS** Web site. You'll find lots of fun facts about beloved cartoonist Charles Schulz and Snoopy and his friends.

IT'S A BIG WORLD, CHARLIE BROWN

BY CHARLES M. SCHULZ

It's a Big World,
Charlie Brown

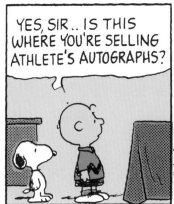
YES, SIR.. IS THIS WHERE YOU'RE SELLING ATHLETE'S AUTOGRAPHS?

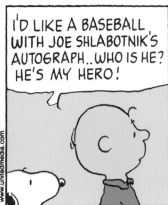
I'D LIKE A BASEBALL WITH JOE SHLABOTNIK'S AUTOGRAPH.. WHO IS HE? HE'S MY HERO!

IS HE HERE? WELL, JUST ASK HIM TO SIGN A BALL, AND I'LL PAY FOR IT..

I USED TO HAVE A LASSIE DOG DISH, BUT SHE NEVER SIGNED IT..

12-30

IS THIS JOE SHLABOTNIK'S AUTOGRAPH? WOW!

WHERE IS HE? MAY I SEE HIM, AND THANK HIM?

WELL, TELL HIM I APPRECIATE THE AUTOGRAPH..

..EVEN THOUGH IT TOOK ALL THE MONEY I'VE GOT..

12-31

WOW! I'LL BE THE ENVY OF EVERY JOE SHLABOTNIK FAN IN THE WORLD!

ALL ONE OF YOU!

SEE? IT'S AN AUTOGRAPHED JOE SHLABOTNIK BASEBALL..

I DON'T THINK SO, CHARLIE BROWN..THIS ISN'T JOE'S SIGNATURE..

1-1-97

IT'S A FORGERY!

GOOD GRIEF!

THEY CHEATED A LITTLE KID! AN INNOCENT, TRUSTING, HERO WORSHIPPING LITTLE KID..

ME!

164

YES, SIR..I THINK YOU SOLD ME A FORGERY.. THIS IS NOT JOE SHLABOTNIK'S SIGNATURE

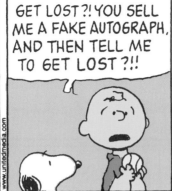
GET LOST?! YOU SELL ME A FAKE AUTOGRAPH, AND THEN TELL ME TO GET LOST?!!

WHAT AM I GOING TO DO ABOUT IT?

1-2-97

LET ME INTRODUCE YOU TO MY WORLD FAMOUS ATTACK DOG..

HEY, KID.. DO YOU WANT A JOB?

A WHAT?

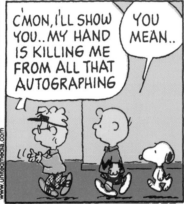
C'MON, I'LL SHOW YOU..MY HAND IS KILLING ME FROM ALL THAT AUTOGRAPHING

YOU MEAN..

SURE! I HAVE TO AUTOGRAPH ALL THIS STUFF, SEE? ARE YOU A GOOD SPELLER?

1-3-97

YESTERDAY, SOMEBODY WANTED A "JOE SHLABOTNIK" OR SOMETHING..GIVE ME A BREAK!

I CAN SPELL SHLABOTNIK

© 1996 United Feature Syndicate, Inc.

..AND YOUR JOB WOULD BE TO HELP ME FORGE THE AUTOGRAPHS ON ALL THESE BATS, AND BALLS, AND PICTURES AND EVERYTHING..

WILL YOU COME TO SEE ME ON VISITOR'S DAY?

1-4-97

165

167

169

I'M TIRED OF ALL THIS KINDERGARTEN STUFF..

WHY DON'T WE RUN AWAY TO PARIS?

IF WE GOT ON A PLANE AT MIDNIGHT, WE COULD BE IN PARIS TOMORROW..

DO YOU HAVE ANY MONEY?

I HAVE FIFTY CENTS..MAYBE WE COULD GET UPGRADED TO BUSINESS CLASS

1-13

THERE'S THIS CUTE LITTLE GIRL WHO SITS NEXT TO ME IN KINDERGARTEN..

1-14

I TOLD HER MAYBE SHE AND I COULD GO TO PARIS SOMEDAY..

I DON'T EVEN KNOW WHERE PARIS IS..

THE TEACHER SAYS THE PRINCIPAL WANTS TO SEE YOU

ME?

1-15

YES, MA'AM..I WAS TOLD THE PRINCIPAL WANTS TO SEE ME

WHY ME? I'M NOBODY..

I DON'T EVEN HAVE A DOG..

170

YES, SIR, MR. PRINCIPAL... WHO? THE LITTLE GIRL WITH THE BRAIDS? SURE, WE'RE IN THE SAME KINDERGARTEN CLASS..

1-16

DID I ASK HER TO GO TO PARIS?

WELL, SURE, BUT THAT WAS JUST A JOKE..

I MEAN, HOW...

HARASSMENT?!!

1-17

IT'S ONLY ME! I'M HOME EARLY..

I'VE BEEN FIRED!

THIS LITTLE GIRL IN MY CLASS WAS SORT OF DEPRESSED, SEE, SO I SAID, "WHY DON'T WE RUN AWAY TO PARIS?" IT WAS A JOKE

SHE THOUGHT IT WAS FUNNY SO SHE TOLD HER MOTHER, WHO TOLD OUR TEACHER, WHO TOLD THE PRINCIPAL, AND I GOT FIRED!

1-18

SUSPENDED   I GUESS SO..

HARASSMENT?   STUPIDITY!

171

SO I GOT SUSPENDED FROM SCHOOL FOR A DAY..

ALL BECAUSE I ASKED A LITTLE GIRL TO GO TO PARIS.. IT WAS JUST A JOKE!

DO YOU THINK I DID WRONG?

SORRY.. I KEEP FORGETTING THAT DOGS CAN'T TALK..

IT'S JUST AS WELL.. I HAVE SOME PRETTY STRONG OPINIONS..

AND THEY HAVE A SECRETARY OF DEFENSE AND A SECRETARY OF AGRICULTURE...

BUT THEY DON'T HAVE A SECRETARY OF BIRDS SO YOU CAN NEVER BE THE SECRETARY OF BIRDS..

YOU'RE RIGHT.. WHO CARES?

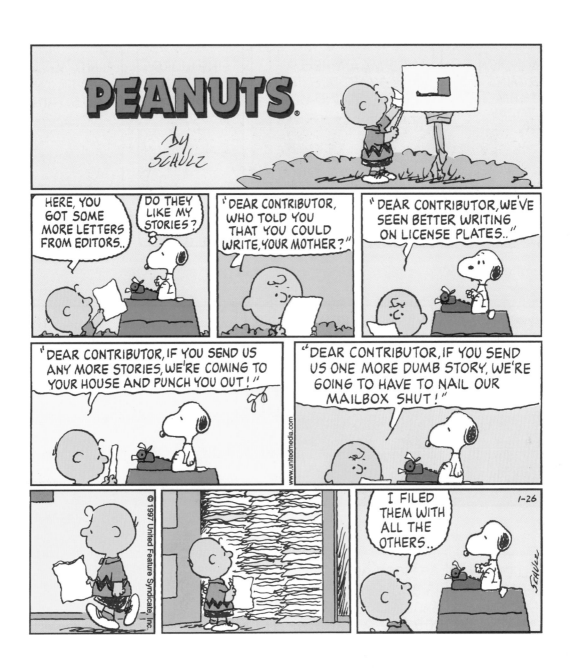

175

YES, MA'AM, I DIDN'T THINK YOU'D MIND IF I BROUGHT HIM TO SCHOOL TODAY..

1-27

YES, MA'AM, HE'S A VERY SMART DOG..THANK YOU FOR SAYING SO..

"FINE WORDS BUTTER NO PARSNIPS"

NO, MA'AM, I NEVER KNOW WHAT HE'S THINKING..

© 1997 United Feature Syndicate, Inc.

www.unitedmedia.com

FOR MY REPORT TODAY I HAVE BROUGHT MY DOG..

YES, HE'S A REAL DOG..NO, IT'S NOT A LITTLE KID IN A DOG SUIT..NO, HE DOESN'T TALK..DOGS DON'T TALK

1-28

ARE THERE ANY OTHER QUESTIONS?

NO, WE'RE NOT GIVING OUT FREE BALLOONS!

© 1997 United Feature Syndicate, Inc.

www.unitedmedia.com

AND I CONCLUDE MY REPORT BY OFFERING THIS SUGGESTION...

AS SOON AS A CHILD IS BORN, HE OR SHE SHOULD BE ISSUED A DOG AND A BANJO..

1-29

MA'AM? THAT'S RIGHT.. A FAMILY OF EIGHT.. EIGHT DOGS AND EIGHT BANJOS..

YES, MA'AM.. WE'RE TALKING HAPPINESS HERE!

© 1997 United Feature Syndicate, Inc.

www.unitedmedia.com

177

Strip 1 (2-3):

WE WERE BEHIND FORTY TO NOTHING! DID WE QUIT? NO!

WE DIDN'T KNOW THE MEANING OF THE WORD "QUIT"!

"QUIT..TO STOP OR DISCONTINUE"

WE LOST THE GAME, AND LEARNED THE MEANING OF THE WORD "QUIT"!

Strip 2 (2-4):

HERE, MARCIE..SHARPEN THIS PENCIL..

SHARPEN IT YOURSELF! WHO ARE YOU, THE FAIRY PRINCESS?

BOY, YOU SURE ARE CRABBY..

WELL, YOU DIDN'T SAY "PLEASE"

HERE, CRABBY.. PLEASE SHARPEN THIS PENCIL..

Strip 3 (2-5):

SIR, DO YOU REALLY THINK I'VE BEEN CRABBY LATELY?

I DON'T KNOW, MARCIE.. IT SEEMS TO ME YOU'RE CRABBY ALL THE TIME..

I THINK THAT'S JUST THE WAY YOU ARE..I TOLERATE YOU BECAUSE I'M THE PATIENT, UNDERSTANDING TYPE

I APPRECIATE YOUR DUMB ATTITUDE, SIR..

179

DO YOU THINK I'M CRABBY, CHARLES?

DO I THINK YOU'RE WHAT?

CRABBY.. YOU KNOW.. ILL TEMPERED

NO, YOU'RE NOT CRABBY AT ALL..

2-6

SEE?

www.unitedmedia.com

WHAT DO YOU KNOW, CHUCK?!

© 1997 United Feature Syndicate, Inc.

SCHULZ

GOOD MORNING, CRABBY..

YOU WANT CRABBY? HERE'S CRABBY!

AAUGH!!

2-7

© 1997 United Feature Syndicate, Inc.

SCHULZ

THAT WAS FUN

YOU'RE CRABBILY WEIRD, MARCIE..

2-8

SCHULZ

© 1997 United Feature Syndicate, Inc.

I WONDER WHAT IT WOULD BE LIKE TO GO ON A LONG TRIP..

LIKE MAYBE TO THE MOUNTAINS..

HOW COULD YOU BE SURE YOU'D HAVE A GOOD TIME?

TAKE YOUR DOG ALONG..

MY PITCHER'S MOUND MAY BE COVERED WITH SNOW, BUT THE MEMORIES ARE STILL HERE..

FORTY TO NOTHING, TWENTY TO NOTHING, FIFTY-THREE TO NOTHING, SIXTY TO NOTHING..

AND THAT GREAT GAME WHEN YOU GOT HIT ON THE HEAD BY A FLY BALL..

I DON'T REMEMBER THAT..

ARE WE GONNA HAVE A BASEBALL TEAM AGAIN THIS YEAR?

2-11

YES, BUT WE WEREN'T GOING TO TELL YOU..

WE WERE ALL HOPING YOU WOULDN'T FIND OUT BECAUSE WE ALL KNOW YOU'RE THE WORST PLAYER IN THE HISTORY OF THE GAME..

PUT ME DOWN FOR RIGHT FIELD

SIGH

I THINK OUR TEAM IS IN TROUBLE THIS YEAR, CHARLIE BROWN..WE'RE WEAK AT EVERY POSITION..

EXCEPT RIGHT FIELD.. SHE'S EXCEPTIONALLY CUTE..

2-12

OUR RIGHT FIELDER IS COMPLETELY HOPELESS..

BUT CUTE..

182

HERE, I MADE YOU A VALENTINE..

SEE? I WROTE A LITTLE POEM, AND THEN I DREW SOME HEARTS AROUND IT..

IT'S IN BLACK AND WHITE..

2-13

IF I HOLD MY HANDS OUT LIKE THIS, YOU CAN PUT A VALENTINE RIGHT IN THEM..

OR YOU CAN STAND LIKE THAT FOR THE REST OF YOUR LIFE, AND NEVER GET ANYTHING..

IT FEELS LIKE IT MIGHT RAIN..

2-14

SOMETIMES I LIE AWAKE AT NIGHT, AND A VOICE ASKS, "DID YOU TAKE YOUR PILLS?"

2-15

SO I SAY, "PILLS? WHAT PILLS? I DON'T TAKE ANY PILLS!"

THEN THE VOICE SAYS, "SORRY, WE CAN'T KEEP TRACK OF EVERYTHING.."

WELL, I'M OFF TO SCHOOL.. I'LL SEE YOU THIS AFTERNOON

IF YOU DECIDE TO GO TO THE MALL, THE KEYS ARE IN THE STATION WAGON..

HE KNOWS I CAN'T SEE OVER THE STEERING WHEEL..

I THINK I'VE DISCOVERED THE SECRET TO LIFE..

YOU JUST HANG AROUND UNTIL YOU GET USED TO IT..

I KNOW WHEN I'M NOT WANTED!

I DON'T HAVE TO STAY HERE

I CAN LEAVE, YOU KNOW!

DON'T FORGET, I'LL BE TWENTY-ONE IN ANOTHER...

..FOURTEEN YEARS!

SEE? AFTER THAT, THINGS IN THE PALACE WERE NEVER THE SAME..

WHAT DO YOU THINK WENT WRONG?

THEY PROBABLY FORGOT TO FEED THE DOG..

YES, SIR..I'D LIKE TO SEE A NEW BASEBALL GLOVE..

COULD I TRY THAT ONE THERE?

I'LL TAKE IT..

I JUST BOUGHT A NEW BASEBALL GLOVE..

I REALLY NEEDED IT.. A GOOD PLAYER NEEDS GOOD EQUIPMENT..

MAYBE IT'LL EVEN IMPROVE YOUR "WON-LOST AGAIN" AVERAGE..

186

DO YOU LIKE ME, CHARLES?

DO I WHAT?

"DO I WHAT?" I WALK ALL THE WAY OVER HERE TO ASK YOU A QUESTION, AND ALL YOU CAN SAY IS, "DO I WHAT?"

2-24

FORGET IT, CHARLES!

FORGET WHAT?

HI, CHARLES..REMEMBER YESTERDAY WHEN I WENT TO YOUR HOUSE?

2-25

I WALKED ALL THE WAY OVER THERE TO ASK YOU IF YOU LIKE ME..

TO DO WHAT?

I CAN'T STAND IT!

I WENT OVER TO SEE CHARLES YESTERDAY..

YOU DID WHAT?

"YOU DID WHAT?" I JUST TOLD YOU! WHY DO YOU ASK ME AGAIN?!

2-26

DOESN'T ANYONE TALK ANYMORE? "COOL!" "NO PROBLEM!" "WHATEVER!" "HOW Y'DOIN'?"

I'M SO DEPRESSED

YOU'RE WHAT?

188

IT'S TOO BAD YOU CAN'T TALK, SNOOPY.. IF YOU COULD, I'LL BET YOU WOULDN'T SAY "COOL," OR "WHATEVER" OR "NO PROBLEM"

I'LL BET YOU'D SAY SOMETHING REALLY WORTHWHILE..

"SOCCER MOM"

SO I'LL ASK YOU AGAIN, CHARLES..DO YOU LIKE ME?

OF COURSE, I LIKE YOU..

WOW!

WELL, THERE'S THIS TV PROGRAM I'M WATCHING, SO...

SO I END UP SITTING ON THE PORCH WITH A DOG..

NO PROBLEM, SWEETIE

IN THE BACK ROW THERE.. LET'S TAKE THE CAP OFF, OKAY?

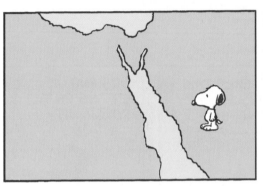

LET'S CHECK THE BOARD, AND SEE WHO YOU PLAY IN THE FIRST ROUND..

OH, NO! YOU PLAY "CRYBABY" BOOBIE! SHE'S THE BIGGEST COMPLAINER AROUND

IT'S TOO COLD TO PLAY TODAY! YESTERDAY IT WAS TOO HOT! THE NET IS TOO HIGH! MY LEG HURTS! MY ELBOW HURTS!

I PROBABLY SHOULD KICK HER.. DOGS ARE ALLOWED TO KICK PEOPLE..

3-3

© 1997 United Feature Syndicate, Inc.

WHAT'S GOING ON?

THIS IS THE FIRST MATCH..SNOOPY'S PLAYING "CRYBABY" BOOBIE..

WHOSE SERVE IS IT? I CAN'T SERVE IN THE SUN! I'LL RECEIVE! THE NET LOOKS TOO HIGH! MY KNEE HURTS! MY EARS HURT!

I THINK I'LL KICK HER..DOGS ARE ALLOWED TO KICK PEOPLE..

3-4

© 1997 United Feature Syndicate, Inc.

WHO'S AHEAD NOW?

I'M NOT SURE..

OUT! THAT BALL WAS OUT!

I CALLED IT OUT BECAUSE I SAW IT OUT SO I CALLED IT OUT! IT WAS WAY OUT!

SHOULD I JUMP OVER THE NET AND KICK HER, OR RUN AROUND THE NET AND KICK HER?

3-5

© 1997 United Feature Syndicate, Inc.

191

OUT! THAT BALL WAS OUT! WAY OUT!

LONG! WAY LONG! WIDE AND LONG! WAY OUT!

LONG! OUT! WAY OUT! OUT! OUT!

LET ME KNOW IF I EVER GET ONE IN..

OUT! OUT!

THAT WAS OUT, WASN'T IT, MOM?

MOM SAID IT WAS OUT!

MY MOM WOULD HAVE CALLED IT "IN".

ANOTHER LOB!

I HATE PLAYING SOMEONE WHO LOBS ALL THE TIME!

THAT WASN'T A LOB.. THAT WAS MY OVERHEAD SMASH!

 WOW! I'M SO TANGLED UP I CAN'T MOVE! COULD YOU GO FOR HELP?

3-9

 WAIT A MINUTE..WHAT I NEED MORE THAN ANYTHING IS A DRINK OF WATER..

 I HATE TO SAY THIS, BUT I DON'T THINK I CAN DRINK OUT OF A DOG DISH..

SCHULZ

I WON! I WON! I'M THE CHAMPION! I WON!!

HEY, MOM! I WON!!

3-10

MOM! I THINK THAT DOG KICKED ME!

I LIKE DOING WATERCOLORS

I HATE IT.. IT'S TOO HARD..

NO, MA'AM.. I HAVEN'T STARTED YET.. I DON'T HAVE ANY WATER..

I DRANK IT..

3-11

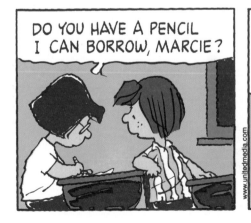

DO YOU HAVE A PENCIL I CAN BORROW, MARCIE?

AND MAYBE SOME PAPER, AND AN ERASER, AND A RULER, AND YOUR MATH BOOK, AND...

MARCIE!

3-12

WHAT DO YOU THINK, MARCIE? I BROUGHT A BANANA IN CASE THEY TEACH US HOW TO MAKE BANANA CREAM PIE TODAY..

3-13

WE DON'T HAVE COOKING CLASSES, SIR..

WE DON'T?

SUGGESTION TIME, MA'AM..LET'S FORGET THE MATH, AND CONCENTRATE ON BANANA CREAM PIE..

YOU'RE BECOMING INCREASINGLY WEIRD, SIR..

© 1997 United Feature Syndicate, Inc.

I'M NOT GOING TO SCHOOL ANYMORE.. THE TEACHER HATES ME, THE PRINCIPAL HATES ME, THE CUSTODIAN HATES ME, THE SCHOOL BOARD HATES ME...

3-14

YOU'D BETTER GET DRESSED..YOU'LL MISS THE SCHOOL BUS..

© 1997 United Feature Syndicate, Inc.

THE BUS DRIVER HATES ME!

3-15

© 1997 United Feature Syndicate, Inc.

PEANUTS by Schulz

IT'S CALLED "PEANUTS GALLERY"

WHAT IS?

A NEW PIECE COMPOSED BY ELLEN TAAFFE ZWILICH.. WE'RE ALL IN IT!

WHAT DO YOU MEAN, WE'RE ALL IN IT?

IT HAS A GREAT BEGINNING.. "SCHROEDER'S BEETHOVEN FANTASY.."

THEN THERE'S "LULLABY FOR LINUS," "SNOOPY DOES THE SAMBA," AND "CHARLIE BROWN'S LAMENT.."

3-16

THEN THERE'S "LUCY FREAKS OUT" AND "PEPPERMINT PATTY AND MARCIE LEAD THE PARADE"!

THE WORLD PREMIERE WILL BE AT CARNEGIE HALL..HERE, LOOK AT IT YOURSELF..

MY PART SHOULD BE LONGER..

A NEW SEASON! THIS IS WHERE I BELONG! THIS IS MY LIFE!

I STAND HERE LIKE THE CAPTAIN OF A SHIP!

3-17

NOTHING CAN SINK THIS VESSEL EXCEPT...

HI, MANAGER! I'M READY TO GO!

..AN ICEBERG!

"PIGPEN," I DON'T UNDERSTAND YOU..

THIS IS THE FIRST INNING OF OUR FIRST GAME, AND YOU'RE ALREADY COVERED WITH DIRT..

3-18

THIS ISN'T ALL FROM TODAY.. SOME OF IT'S LEFT OVER FROM LAST YEAR..

DO ME A FAVOR..GO ASK "PIGPEN" WHY HE DOESN'T WEAR A BASEBALL CAP..

THE MANAGER WANTS TO KNOW WHY YOU DON'T WEAR A CAP..

3-19

HE SAID HE DOESN'T WANT TO MUSS UP HIS HAIR..

197

"PIGPEN," WHY CAN'T YOU LOOK NEAT LIKE THE OTHER PLAYERS?

LAST YEAR I BATTED .712

3-20

NEATNESS DOESN'T BAT .712!

WAP!

"PIGPEN" SLIDES INTO HOME! HE'S SAFE! HE'S GETTING UP! HE'S DUSTING HIMSELF OFF..

WHY?

3-21

REMEMBER, IF A FLY BALL COMES YOUR WAY, DON'T FORGET TO ALLOW FOR THE WIND!

I'M WORKING ON IT!

3-22

200

201

YOU CAN COME OUT WHEN YOU LEARN TO BEHAVE!

3-30

HELLO? THIS IS "RERUN".. OH, HI, GRAMMA.. HOW ARE YOU?

I'M FINE, THANK YOU.. KINDERGARTEN?

YES, I'M DOING FINE KINDERGARTENWISE..

YOU KNOW WHAT I'D LIKE TO DO? I'D LIKE TO TELL YOU THAT THE LITTLE RED-HAIRED GIRL IS AT THE DOOR, AND THEN, WHEN YOU RUN TO SEE HER, I'D YELL, "APRIL FOOL!"

THAT'S WHAT I'D REALLY LIKE TO DO..

BY THE WAY, THERE'S A GIANT LIZARD CRAWLING UP YOUR BACK..

AAUGH!

APRIL FOOL!

I HEAR YOU MADE AN IMPASSIONED SPEECH TO THE JURY YESTERDAY..

DID IT BRING TEARS TO THEIR EYES?

NO, THEY FELL ASLEEP

203

AAUGH!!

WHAT'D YOU DO THAT FOR?!

I DIDN'T MEAN TO.. IT WAS A DOG THING..

I HATE TO TELL YOU THIS, MA'AM, BUT THE ROOF IS LEAKING AGAIN..

NO, I CAN'T GIVE YOU MY HOMEWORK BECAUSE IT'S IN MY BINDER WHICH IS KEEPING ME FROM DROWNING..

WHEN YOU SIGH, MA'AM, IT REMINDS ME OF A BREEZE WEAVING ITS WAY THROUGH THE PINES..

..AND WHEN AN ACTIVITY GETS OUT OF HAND, IT CAN BECOME A COMPULSION..

PSYCHIATRIC HELP 5¢

THE DOCTOR IS IN

ANYONE FOR "OLD MAID"? ONE MORE GAME? ANYONE? COME ON..ANYONE?

YES, MA'AM, I THINK OUR ROOF IS LEAKING AGAIN..

IS IT KEEPING ME AWAKE?

4-7

SARCASM DOES NOT BECOME YOU, MA'AM..

© 1997 United Feature Syndicate, Inc.

www.unitedmedia.com

SIR, THE ROOF IS LEAKING AGAIN, AND YOU'RE GETTING ALL WET..

I DON'T LIKE TO COMPLAIN, MARCIE..

4-8

THEN I'LL DO IT FOR YOU!

WE WERE JUST WONDERING, MA'AM, IF PERCHANCE YOU MIGHT HAVE NOTICED...

THE ROOF IS LEAKING!

© 1997 United Feature Syndicate, Inc.

www.unitedmedia.com

THIS IS HOW IT IS, MR. PRINCIPAL..

HALF THE KIDS IN OUR CLASS CAN'T READ, AND HALF CAN'T MULTIPLY 6X8..

NONE OF THEM EVER HEARD OF BOSNIA, AND COULDN'T TELL YOU WHO WROTE "HAMLET"

4-9

I TALKED TO THE PRINCIPAL, SIR..

WHAT'D HE SAY ABOUT THE ROOF LEAKING?

I FORGOT TO MENTION IT..

© 1997 United Feature Syndicate, Inc.

GOOD NEWS, SIR..THE PRINCIPAL ASKED THE CUSTODIAN TO CLIMB UP, AND FIX THE LEAK IN THE ROOF..

4-10

HOWEVER, YOU MAY HAVE TO WAIT A WHILE LONGER...

THE CUSTODIAN FELL OFF THE ROOF!

HOW ABOUT THAT, MARCIE.. I THINK THEY FIXED THE LEAK IN THE ROOF..

4-11

LET'S JUST HOPE THERE AREN'T SOME OTHER PLACES WHERE...

IT'S A WATER DISH..WHAT DID YOU THINK IT WAS?

?

SURE, GO AHEAD.. HAVE A DRINK..

4-12

NO, I DON'T HAVE ANY PAPER CUPS..

207

YOUR JOB WILL BE TO HOLD THE KITE..

DOES MY JOB HAVE A TITLE?

CALL YOURSELF ANYTHING YOU WANT.. JUST LET GO OF THE KITE AFTER I START RUNNING..

I CAN BE THE "KITE ASSISTANT.."

OR MAYBE "HEAD KITE ASSISTANT." OR EVEN "CHIEF KITE ASSISTANT."

RIP!

4-13

HOW ABOUT "EX-KITE ASSISTANT FOURTH CLASS"?

I CAN'T STAND IT! I JUST CAN'T STAND IT!

IF SHE READS TO US AGAIN ABOUT DICK AND JANE, I'LL GO CRAZY..

4-14

YES, MA'AM, I THINK THE CLASS MIGHT LIKE TO HEAR THE PART WHERE ANNA KARENINA THROWS HERSELF UNDER THE TRAIN..

ALL RIGHT, LET'S HEAR HOW DICK AND JANE ARE DOING..

I HAVE ANOTHER NEW PHILOSOPHY..

"WHAT DID YOU EXPECT, A MEDAL?"

4-15

SOME PHILOSOPHIES TAKE A THOUSAND YEARS..I THINK OF THEM IN TWO MINUTES..

ALL RIGHT, WHO TOOK THE LAST COOKIE?!

IN FACT, WHO TOOK THE FIRST COOKIE?!

4-16

I TOOK THE TWELFTH ONE..

209

NATURE HIKES ARE IMPORTANT..

THEY'RE IMPORTANT BECAUSE WE NEED TO BE ACQUAINTED WITH OUR SURROUNDINGS

4-17

WE NEED TO LEARN THE NAMES OF THE TREES, THE MOUNTAINS, THE LAKES, THE BIRDS..

© 1997 United Feature Syndicate, Inc.
www.unitedmedia.com

YES, I KNOW YOUR NAME IS "BILL"

GUESS WHAT..IN KINDERGARTEN TODAY WE LEARNED TO TIE OUR SHOES..

I THINK I'M PRETTY GOOD AT IT..I'M A FAST LEARNER

© 1997 United Feature Syndicate, Inc.
www.unitedmedia.com

4-18
THOSE AREN'T YOUR SHOES!

JUST CHECKING IN, MANAGER..

4-19

JUST LETTING YOU KNOW EVERYTHING IS TAKEN CARE OF OUT IN RIGHT FIELD..

© 1997 United Feature Syndicate, Inc.
www.unitedmedia.com

I ABSOLUTELY REFUSE TO ASK WHAT THAT'S ALL ABOUT..

4-21

SEE? I'M DRAWING A LANDSCAPE..

IT NEEDS A WATERFALL, AND A MOUNTAIN, AND A DEER STANDING IN A MEADOW, AND A SUNSET, AND A TINY LOG CABIN, AND A STREAM WITH A TROUT JUMPING OUT OF THE WATER..

AND A BORDER COLLIE HERDING SOME SHEEP..

© 1997 United Feature Syndicate, Inc.

It was a dark and stormy night.

NO, NOT AGAIN..

4-22

© 1997 United Feature Syndicate, Inc.

It was one of those dark nights when you weren't sure if it was going to be stormy or not.

Gentlemen, Enclosed please find my latest short story.

4-23

© 1997 United Feature Syndicate, Inc.

212

No, ma'am, I raised my left hand..

When I raise my left hand, it means I'm not sure, but when I raise my right hand, it means I'm sure..

See? This time I raised my left hand..

Ma'am, where are you going? **Come back!**

4-24

Here you are, sir... enjoy your meal..

Sigh

Dogs don't give tips..

4-25

4-26

Don't feel bad.. I'll get one for you tomorrow..

WHY CAN'T I HAVE A NORMAL TEAM LIKE EVERYONE ELSE?

YES, MA'AM..READ US AGAIN ABOUT THE CLUMSY KID WHO FELL DOWN THE RABBIT HOLE..

"ALICE"

AND ABOUT THE CHESAPEAKE CAT..

© 1997 United Feature Syndicate, Inc.

"CHESHIRE"

AND ABOUT HOW SHE MET TIGER WOODS..

4-28

SHE NEVER MET TIGER WOODS..

READ US ANYTHING YOU WANT, MA'AM..

I'M GETTING YOUR SUPPER AS FAST AS I CAN!

www.unitedmedia.com

I KNOW YOU'RE HUNGRY, BUT YOU DON'T HAVE TO BREAK THE DOOR DOWN!

4-29

© 1997 United Feature Syndicate, Inc.

I DON'T THINK I SHOULD GO TO SCHOOL ANYMORE..

www.unitedmedia.com

INSTEAD OF GETTING SMARTER, I'M GETTING DUMBER EVERY DAY..

© 1997 United Feature Syndicate, Inc.

I FIGURE IN ABOUT ONE MORE MONTH I'LL BOTTOM OUT..

4-30

YOU GOT HERE FAST.. WHEN DID YOU LEAVE?

THE BIG WING WAS ON TWO, AND THE SMALL WING WAS ON NINE?

SOMEDAY YOU SHOULD LEARN TO TELL TIME..

FLOWERS FOR THE TEACHER?

WHAT ARE YOU TRYING TO DO, MARCIE, GET TO BE AN OFFICER?

DON'T FORGET THE ENLISTED MEN, MA'AM..

BEETHOVEN COULD HAVE GOT MORE WORK DONE IF HE HADN'T HAD TO WORRY ABOUT HIS NEPHEW..

I DIDN'T HAVE ANY COLD CEREAL THIS MORNING BECAUSE MY STUPID BROTHER USED UP ALL THE MILK!

WHAT DO BALL PLAYERS TALK ABOUT WHEN THEY MEET OUT ON THE MOUND?

DON'T ASK!

MY LIFE IS LIKE A COLORING BOOK! EACH DAY I HAVE A NEW PAGE WITH NEW PICTURES TO COLOR..

BEING VERY CAREFUL, OF COURSE, TO STAY INSIDE THE LINES..

MY LIFE IS LIKE A MESSY COLORING BOOK..

IT IS DAWN.. HERE'S THE WORLD WAR I FLYING ACE WALKING OUT ONTO THE AERODROME...

HIS FAITHFUL MECHANICS WILL HAVE HIS PLANE FUELED AND READY TO GO..

AS SOON AS THEY FINISH PLAYING THIS HAND..

AS THE WORLD WAR I FLYING ACE TAKES OFF, HE SEES THE WORRIED LOOKS ON THE FACES OF HIS FAITHFUL MECHANICS..

HE KNOWS THEY WILL THINK OF NOTHING ELSE UNTIL HE RETURNS

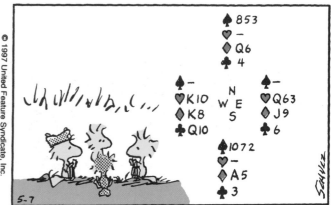

HERE'S THE WORLD WAR I FLYING ACE RETURNING TO THE AERODROME...

HE KNOWS HIS FAITHFUL MECHANICS WILL JUMP UP AND DOWN AND CHEER WHEN THEY SEE HIM LAND..

5-8

♠ K10 7
♥ 984
♦ AJ10 8
♣ Q73

♠ J43   ♠ 82
♥ AQ10763   ♥ J
♦ —   N   ♦ Q7652
♣ K1096 W E ♣ J8542
         S

♠ AQ965
♥ K52
♦ K943
♣ A

WHAT KIND OF FAITHFUL MECHANICS ARE YOU?!

5-9

THERE I WAS, OFF FIGHTING THE RED BARON, WHILE YOU GUYS WERE PLAYING BRIDGE!

WHAT DO YOU HAVE TO SAY FOR YOURSELVES?

www.unitedmedia.com

WELL, WITH THREE KINGS, I'D HAVE GONE RIGHT TO SIX SPADES..

SOMETIMES I LIE AWAKE AT NIGHT, AND I ASK, "DOES ANYONE REMEMBER ME?"

5-10

THEN A VOICE COMES TO ME OUT OF THE DARK THAT SAYS, "SURE, FRANK, WE REMEMBER YOU"

219

SAY WE'VE BEEN MARRIED FOR ABOUT SIX MONTHS...

AND LET'S SAY I'VE MADE A BEAUTIFUL TUNA CASSEROLE FOR DINNER...

YOU WALK INTO THE KITCHEN, AND YOU SAY, "WHAT, TUNA CASSEROLE AGAIN?"

I'D NEVER SAY THAT..

THEN I SAY, "I WORKED HARD MAKING THIS CASSEROLE, BUT ALL YOU CARE ABOUT IS THAT STUPID PIANO!"

5-11

THEN YOU WALK OUT..

SORRY I'M LATE..I GOT INVOLVED IN A MARITAL DISPUTE..

I NEVER KNOW WHAT ANYONE IS TALKING ABOUT..

I NEED HELP WITH MY HOMEWORK..

WE ALL NEED HELP WITH OUR HOMEWORK..WE'RE ALL PLEADING FOR SOMEONE TO LISTEN..WE'RE ALL DESPERATE

5-12

I LIVE IN THE WRONG HOUSE..

NO, THAT'S NOT A STAR..IT'S A COMET..

5-13

HOW DO I KNOW? IT SAYS SO ON THE SIDE..

HE NEVER BELIEVES ANY-THING I TELL HIM..

COME ON, CHARLIE BROWN, STRIKE THIS GUY OUT! YOU CAN DO IT!

5-14

WHAT CAN I SAY?

YES, MA'AM..I'M WRITING A STORY..

IT'S ABOUT THIS KID WHO'S IN KINDERGARTEN, AND HOW THE STRESS IS SLOWLY DESTROYING HIM..

EVERY MORNING HE...

MA'AM?

5-15

WELL, I HAVE ANOTHER ONE HERE ABOUT SOME PURPLE BUNNIES..

SOMEWHERE IN THIS GREAT CITY THERE HAS TO BE A MAILBOX WITH A LOVE LETTER FOR ME

BUT THIS ISN'T IT..

STUPID MAILBOX!

5-16

STUPID KID!

OKAY, LUCY, STAND WAY BACK THERE BY THOSE BUSHES..

5-17

I'M GONNA HIT YOU A FLY BALL..

TRY TO GET IT BACK AS FAST AS YOU CAN

IT'S IN HERE SOMEPLACE..

222

LIKE I'VE SAID BEFORE, NEVER TAKE A SHORTCUT THROUGH A MINIATURE GOLF COURSE..

NO, MA'AM, BUT I CAN MAKE A WILD GUESS...

5-19

"ZEBRAS"! I'LL SAY "ZEBRAS"!

SIR, THE ANSWER IS "TWELVE.."

"TWELVE ZEBRAS"!

HERE'S THE WORLD FAMOUS PATRIOT SOLDIER STANDING GUARD AT VALLEY FORGE..

5-20

"THESE ARE THE TIMES THAT TRY MEN'S SOULS"

TO PUT IT ANOTHER WAY, "I HOPE I MAKE THE CUT"

HEY, MARCIE..I UNDERSTAND THERE'S A RUMOR GOING AROUND THAT I MAY BE NAMED "OUTSTANDING STUDENT OF THE YEAR"

THAT'S INTERESTING, SIR.. I HEARD ANOTHER RUMOR THAT THE MOON IS GOING TO FALL OUT OF THE SKY..

5-21

I'M HANGING UP, MARCIE..

MORALE IS LOW AT VALLEY FORGE..

5-22

THE TROOPS ARE HUNGRY.. NOTHING TO EAT BUT FIRECAKE AND WATER..

AND THIS MORNING GENERAL WASHINGTON GAVE US MORE BAD NEWS...

WE'RE ALL OUT OF GRAPE JELLY!

© 1997 United Feature Syndicate, Inc.

SEE, MARCIE? HERE ARE THE NAMES OF EVERYONE WHO'S UP FOR "OUTSTANDING STUDENT OF THE YEAR".. THERE'S MY NAME, SEE?

I COUNTED THEM, SIR.. YOU'RE FOUR HUNDREDTH ON THE LIST..

FOUR HUNDREDTH AND MOVING UP FAST!

5-23

I NEED HELP WITH MY HOMEWORK..

AGAIN?

5-24

I HOPE YOU APPRECIATE THIS..

CALL ME IF YOU EVER NEED YOUR SHOES TIED..

© 1997 United Feature Syndicate, Inc.

225

FLY? SURE, I KNOW BIRDS CAN FLY..

WHAT'S SO GREAT ABOUT THAT?

DOGS CAN DO A LOT OF THINGS BIRDS CAN'T DO..

DOGS CAN BARK!

5-25

WOOF!

IT'S ANOTHER COLD DAY AT VALLEY FORGE..I'VE BAKED GENERAL WASHINGTON A PIECE OF FIRECAKE..

5-26

HE SAYS TO ME, "WHERE'S THE GRAPE JELLY?" I TELL HIM WE HAVEN'T HAD GRAPE JELLY FOR SIX WEEKS..

THEN HE SAYS,"CAN'T SOMEONE GO OVER TO THE MALL,AND GET SOME?"

IT WAS TOO HARD TO EXPLAIN

© 1997 United Feature Syndicate, Inc.

CAN YOU BELIEVE IT, CHUCK? CAN YOU BELIEVE IT?

BELIEVE WHAT?

MARCIE WAS NAMED "OUTSTANDING STUDENT OF THE YEAR"! I THOUGHT I WAS GOING TO WIN!

5-27

I'VE NEVER BEEN SO DEPRESSED IN ALL MY LIFE..

YOU SHOULD HAVE BEEN AT VALLEY FORGE..

© 1997 United Feature Syndicate, Inc.

OH, SURE, MARCIE..STAND OUT IN FRONT OF MY HOUSE WITH YOUR STUPID TROPHY!

I JUST THOUGHT YOU'D LIKE TO CONGRATULATE ME.. AND MAYBE SHARE IN MY GLORY...

5-28

YOU THINK I'M JEALOUS, DON'T YOU? WELL, I'M NOT JEALOUS!

I MEAN, I'M LIKE NOT TOTALLY JEALOUS!

© 1997 United Feature Syndicate, Inc.

227

WHY WASN'T I NAMED "OUTSTANDING STUDENT OF THE YEAR," CHUCK? TELL ME WHY, CHUCK..

5-29

MAYBE BECAUSE YOU FALL ASLEEP IN CLASS EVERY DAY..

YOU DON'T LIKE ME, DO YOU, CHUCK?

I'M JUST TRYING TO EXPLAIN WHY YOU PROBABLY...

Z

YES, MA'AM..I KNOW I DIDN'T MAKE "OUTSTANDING STUDENT OF THE YEAR".. I KNOW I DIDN'T WIN...

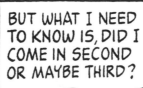

BUT WHAT I NEED TO KNOW IS, DID I COME IN SECOND OR MAYBE THIRD?

5-30

FOUR HUNDREDTH?!

PROBABLY A LOT CLOSER THAN IT SOUNDS, HUH, MA'AM?

I SUPPOSE HAVING A DOG HELPS TO MAKE YOU FEEL BETTER WHEN YOU'RE DEPRESSED, HUH, CHUCK?

I WOULDN'T KNOW..

SAY "GOODBYE" TO VALLEY FORGE, MEN.. WE'RE MOVING OUT!

5-31

228

229

THIS IS MY FAVORITE PROGRAM..

WHY? ALL THEY'RE DOING IS DANCING..

I LIKE TO WATCH OLD PEOPLE HAVING FUN..

WHERE'S EVERYBODY GOING? COME BACK!

YOU DON'T SEE ME LEAVING, DO YOU? YOU DON'T SEE OUR SHORTSTOP LEAVING, DO YOU?

AND MISS ALL THE FUN?!

A KID THREW A TANTRUM TODAY IN KINDERGARTEN..

HE KICKED AND SCREAMED AND WOULDN'T GET UP OFF THE FLOOR..

I FINALLY HAD TO TALK TO HIM MYSELF...

YOU'D BETTER GET UP RIGHT NOW, KID, BEFORE THE ZAMBONI RUNS OVER YOU!

HE GOT UP!

230

YES, MA'AM, OUR FIRST YEAR IN KINDERGARTEN HAS GONE BY FAST..

6-5

I SUPPOSE YOU'LL BE AWAY ALL SUMMER, WON'T YOU?

IS THERE A NUMBER WHERE WE COULD REACH YOU?

JUNE 6, 1944, "TO REMEMBER"

WHAT ARE YOU DOING HERE? I THOUGHT YOU WANTED TO SEE THE COWBOY MOVIE..

6-7

I DID, BUT LUCY WANTS TO SEE THIS SPACE MOVIE..

WE TOOK A VOTE...

I LOST, ONE TO ONE..

LOOK, MARCIE.. I READ THE BOOK, AND I WROTE THE REPORT!

I'M GONNA HAND IT IN TODAY..

SCHOOL IS OUT, SIR.. IT'S VACATION TIME

OUT?

SCHOOL IS OUT?

UNTIL SEPTEMBER..

6-8

BUT I READ THE BOOK! I WROTE THE REPORT!

THE SCHOOL IS CLOSED, SIR..THERE'S NO ONE THERE EXCEPT THE CUSTODIAN..

www.unitedmedia.com

ANYONE WANT TO HEAR A GOOD BOOK REPORT?

CUSTODIAN

THIS LOOKS LIKE A GOOD CAMP..

NO, IT DOESN'T

IT'S RIGHT BY A LAKE

WHO CARES?

AND NEAR SOME MOUNTAINS

HILLS

AND THEY HAVE HORSES

ONE HORSE

THEY SAY THE FOOD IS GOOD

COLD CEREAL

WELL, SHALL WE GO THERE?

WHY NOT?

I HEAR YOU'VE DECIDED NOT TO GO TO SUMMER CAMP AFTER ALL..

WHEN YOU HAVE A DOG, YOU SHOULD STAY HOME, AND MAKE YOUR DOG HAPPY.. THAT'S WHAT YOU SHOULD DO.. YOU SHOULD STAY HOME..

EXCEPT FOR THOSE OBVIOUSLY NECESSARY SHORT TRIPS IN TO BUY DOG FOOD..

6-10

I THINK I HEARD SOMEONE AT THE DOOR..

IT'S PROBABLY NOBODY IMPORTANT

YOU'RE RIGHT..

WE'RE HARDLY IMPORTANT AT ALL..

6-11

233

ANDY! OLAF! WHAT ARE YOU GUYS DOING HERE?

WE LEFT THE FARM.. WE DIDN'T FIT IN..

WE'RE LOOKING FOR A NEW HOME..

WE THOUGHT YOU MIGHT BE ABLE TO TELL US WHERE OUR KIND WOULD FIT IN...

SOMETIMES I THINK ABOUT MY BROTHERS, ANDY AND OLAF... I WONDER WHAT THEY'RE DOING NOW..

6-12

I'VE COME TO OFFER YOU A FREE DOG..

HE NEEDS A HOME, AND YOU NEED HIS COMFORTING COMPANIONSHIP..

HE COMES FROM A LONG LINE OF CHAMPIONS... YOU WANT A DOG? HERE IS JUST THE DOG FOR YOU!

WHERE?

6-13

I'VE COME TO OFFER YOU A FREE DOG.. HIS NAME IS "OLAF"

DOES HE BITE?

ONLY IF ATTACKED BY A PIZZA..

CAN HE DO TRICKS?

HE'S DOING ONE NOW..

6-14

HE'S STANDING ON THE PORCH WITHOUT FALLING OFF..

235

HOW WOULD YOU LIKE TO HAVE A FREE DOG? THIS IS ANDY AND THIS IS OLAF..

MOM SAYS DOGS ARE TOO MUCH TROUBLE, THEY BARK TOO MUCH, AND OUR YARD ISN'T BIG ENOUGH..

WELL, AT LEAST SHE DIDN'T SAY ANYTHING ABOUT PREFERRING CATS

MOM SAYS DO YOU HAPPEN TO HAVE A CAT ?

6-16

MAYBE YOU GUYS SHOULD GO VISIT OUR BROTHER SPIKE IN THE DESERT..HE KNOWS MICKEY MOUSE..

MICKEY MOUSE HAS A LOT OF FRIENDS IN HOLLYWOOD..

6-17

I'LL BET HE COULD GET YOU JOBS AT ONE OF THE STUDIOS.. HOW DOES THAT SOUND?

WHO'S MICKEY MOUSE ?

I WROTE TO SPIKE SO HE'LL BE EXPECTING YOU

REMEMBER, THE MOON IS ALWAYS OVER HOLLYWOOD SO JUST FOLLOW THE MOON..

6-18

THE LAST TIME WE WENT SOMEPLACE, HE TOLD US THE NORTH STAR IS ALWAYS OVER MINNEAPOLIS..

About a month after Andy and Olaf left, I received a note from Spike.

He said Andy and Olaf never arrived.

I remember saying goodbye to them that morning.

6-19

That's the last time we ever saw them.

I THOUGHT WE WERE GOING TO BIBLE CAMP..

IT GOT CANCELED

YOU MEAN I MEMORIZED ALL THOSE BIBLE VERSES FOR NOTHING?

6-20

"JESUS WEPT" "REMEMBER LOT'S WIFE"

I CAN DO LONGER ONES, TOO..

"THOU ART THE MAN!" "LET MY PEOPLE GO!"

THAT OTHER TEAM IS TRASH-TALKING US, CHARLIE BROWN..

I GOT EVEN WITH THEM, THOUGH...

6-21

I SAID, "YOU GUYS THINK YOU'RE SO GREAT..MOZART WAS WRITING SYMPHONIES WHEN HE WAS YOUR AGE!"

THAT REALLY SHUT 'EM UP..

I'LL BET IT DID..

237

239

I DON'T THINK YOU'RE BEING FAIR TO CHARLES, SIR..

ONE DAY YOU TELL HIM WE'RE NOT THINKING OF HIM ..THE NEXT DAY YOU TELL HIM WE MISS HIM..

YOU'RE PLAYING LOVERS' GAMES, SIR

LOVERS AREN'T REAL PEOPLE, MARCIE..

JUNK MAIL! ALL WE EVER GET IS JUNK MAIL!

HERE, WE GOT SOME JUNK MAIL WITH YOUR NAME ON IT...

"WE MISS YOU, AND WE THINK OF YOU NIGHT AND DAY"... AND IT'S ON PINK STATIONERY..

PROBABLY A TIRE COMPANY OR SOMETHING

HI, CHUCK..IS THAT YOU? I'M CALLING BECAUSE MARCIE SAYS I HAVEN'T BEEN FAIR WITH YOU...

SHE SAYS I TELL YOU WE DON'T THINK ABOUT YOU, AND THEN THAT WE ACTUALLY MISS YOU

HAVE I BEEN UNFAIR, CHUCK? WHAT DO YOU THINK? TELL ME..

WOOF!

240

HEY, CHUCK..WE'RE BACK FROM CAMP! DID YOU LIKE MY LETTER?

I POURED MY HEART INTO THAT LETTER, CHUCK..

6-30

I WANTED YOU TO KNOW THAT EVEN THOUGH WE WERE FAR AWAY, YOU WERE IN OUR THOUGHTS.. KIND OF POETIC, HUH?

ANYWAY, CHUCK..DID YOU LIKE MY LETTER?

WHAT LETTER?

WHAT LETTER?! WHAT DO YOU MEAN, WHAT LETTER?!

I WROTE YOU A LOVE LETTER, CHUCK! I WROTE IT ON PINK STATIONERY!!

7-1

IS THAT WHAT THAT WAS? I THOUGHT IT WAS JUNK MAIL SO I THREW IT AWAY..

AAUGH!

A JUNK MAIL LOVE LETTER! HA HA HA HA!!

CHARLES THOUGHT YOUR LOVE LETTER WAS JUNK MAIL SO HE THREW IT AWAY! HA HA HA HA HA!!

YOU SHOULDN'T BE LAUGHING, MARCIE.. YOU SHOULD BE FEELING SORRY FOR ME

HOW'S THIS, SIR? SEE? I'M FEELING SORRY FOR YOU..

7-2

JUNK MAIL! HA HA HA HA!

I CAN'T STAND IT..

I GUESS I LEARNED SOMETHING, MARCIE..A BROKEN HEART STAYS WITH YOU FOREVER...

7-3

NEVER GIVE YOUR HEART TO A BLOCKHEAD..

THAT'S GOOD ADVICE, SIR.. I'LL REMEMBER THAT, SIR..

BONK!

I HIT YOU ON THE HEAD SO I THINK THAT MEANS YOU GET A FREE SHOT...

BONK!

7-4

I'VE OFTEN WONDERED IF YOU CAN SEE THE OCEAN FROM THERE..

7-5

NO? THEN I THINK YOU CAN TAKE THE LIFE JACKET OFF..

243

AND THANKS FOR LETTING YOUR DOG COME OUT AND PLAY WITH ME..

THIS IS THE GAME I'VE INVENTED, AND HERE ARE THE RULES..

I'LL THROW THE BALL, AND YOU'LL CATCH IT, OKAY?

7-6

IF YOU CATCH IT ON THE FIRST BOUNCE, YOU GET THREE POINTS..

TWO BOUNCES, YOU GET TWO POINTS.. THREE BOUNCES, ONE POINT..IF YOU DON'T CATCH IT, I GET TEN POINTS...

THERE WAS ONE OTHER RULE, TOO, BUT I'VE FORGOTTEN WHAT IT WAS...

NOW I REMEMBER.. NO BODY CHECKING!

I REMEMBER WHEN MICKEY MOUSE GAVE ME THESE NICE YELLOW SHOES...

7-7

I WANTED TO DO SOMETHING FOR HIM IN RETURN TO SHOW MY APPRECIATION...

I OFFERED HIM MY HAT, BUT IT WOULDN'T FIT OVER HIS EARS..

SORRY I MISSED THAT ONE, MANAGER.. YOU HAVE MY HEARTFELT APOLOGY..

I'D RATHER HAVE YOU CATCH ONE FLY BALL THAN HAVE FIFTY HEARTFELT APOLOGIES!

HOW ABOUT FIFTY APOLOGIES, BUT WE LEAVE OUT THE HEARTFELTS?

7-8

THE GOVERNMENT'S "MIDNIGHT BASKETBALL" PROGRAM HAS STILL TO REACH SOME OUTLYING AREAS..

7-9

© 1997 United Feature Syndicate, Inc.

245

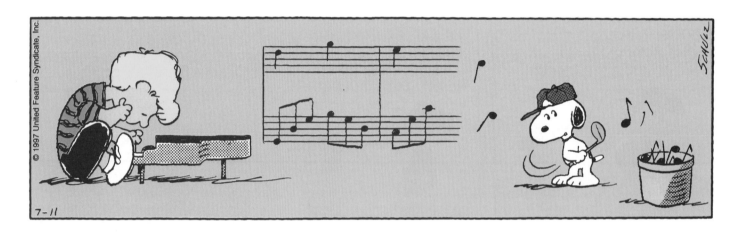

PEANUTS *by Schulz*

C'MON, CHARLIE BROWN..STRIKE OUT THE FAT KID!

THAT'S OKAY.. LET'S GET THE SKINNY KID!

HEY, CEMENT HEAD! WHO SAID YOU COULD HIT?!

HEY, NOODLE NECK! YOU SWING LIKE MY GRANDMOTHER!

WELL, WE LOST AGAIN.. BY THE WAY, SOME OF THEIR PLAYERS WANT TO TALK TO YOU..

PLAYERS? WHAT PLAYERS?

7-13

THE FAT KID, THE SKINNY KID, CEMENT HEAD, AND NOODLE NECK..

I THINK I'LL GO HOME A DIFFERENT WAY..

I'M GETTING SO I DON'T TRUST ANYBODY..

YOU DON'T EVEN TRUST ME?

I TRUST YOU ABOUT AS FAR AS YOU CAN THROW THAT BLANKET..

7-14

MY SISTER TRUSTS ME EIGHT FEET..

WHAT'S LONGER THAN A LINE THAT STRETCHES AROUND THE WORLD?

A LINE FROM HERE TO THE SUN?

7-15

NO, A SUMMER READING LIST..

MARCIE, WHAT DO I DO AFTER I FINISH READING THE BOOKS ON THIS LIST?

WRITE A REPORT ON EACH ONE..

SURE, MARCIE..

7-16

TELL THE TEACHER HOW MUCH YOU LIKED THEM..

SURE, MARCIE..

DOGS ARE LUCKY.. DOGS DON'T HAVE TO WASTE THEIR SUMMER READING "SILAS MARNER"

I READ A BOOK ABOUT A CAT ONCE..

I READ IT WHEN I WAS GOING TO OBEDIENCE SCHOOL..

"SILAS MARNER" IS ON OUR "REQUIRED READING" LIST..

SO WAS THE CAT BOOK..

7-17

OKAY, MARCIE, I'VE FINISHED READING "SILAS MARNER".. NOW, WHAT DO I DO?

NOW, YOU WRITE YOUR REPORT..

YOU'RE KIDDING.. ON THE BOOK?

WHY NOT? DID YOU ACTUALLY READ IT?

YES, BUT I DIDN'T PAY ANY ATTENTION..

7-18

LOOK, I FOUND A LIST OF THE PLAYERS ON THE OTHER TEAM..

"CLAY, BLAKE, MORGAN, TRAVIS, TRENT, HUNTER.."

"BAILEY, MADISON, TAYLOR AND JUSTIN"

NOBODY'S NAMED BILL ANYMORE..

7-19

249

EXCUSE ME.. CAN ANYONE TELL ME IF MY PLANE IS READY?

YES, I CAN SEE THIS IS AN IMPORTANT HAND..

♠KJ7
♥AK109
♦J87
♣AJ5

♠3   ♠1098542
♥7632   N   ♥Q
♦1094 W   E   ♦AKQ62
♣Q7642   S   ♣9

    ♠AQ6
    ♥J854
    ♦53
    ♣K1083

NO, I REALIZE YOU'RE NOT PLAYING "OLD MAID"

7-21

I HEARD YOU! YOU DON'T HAVE TO YELL AT ME!

I WASN'T YELLING... I WAS EXPRESSING MYSELF FORCEFULLY!

7-22

LET'S TRY GOING BACK TO YELLING..

GO AWAY, DOG!

7-23

AAUGH!

FAKED HER OUT!

252

253

I DON'T KNOW... I SURE DON'T SEE IT..

I'LL RUN BACK TO THE PRO SHOP, AND ASK THEM..

7-28

HAS ANYONE TURNED IN A CHEESEBURGER?

I'M KICKING THIS BEACH BALL CLEAR ACROSS THE OCEAN WHERE SOME OTHER LITTLE KID CAN FIND IT..

THIS IS A LAKE..

7-29

SOMEBODY BETTER TELL THAT KID..

WHAT ARE YOU LOOKING AT?

I'M LOOKING FOR PIRATE SHIPS..

7-30

I THINK MAYBE I SEE ONE..

WHERE? I DON'T SEE A THING..

RIGHT OUT THERE..

BUT I CAN'T TELL..IT'S EITHER A PIRATE SHIP OR A ZAMBONI..

254

A PIRATE SHIP! I SEE A PIRATE SHIP!

HERE'S BLACKBEAGLE, THE WORLD FAMOUS PIRATE, LEADING HIS SCURVY BAND ASHORE...

7-31

SOMEBODY TELL CONRAD HE'S ONLY SUPPOSED TO WEAR ONE EYE PATCH..

BONK!

SOME PIRATES JUST LANDED ON THE BEACH! A REAL NASTY LOOKING BUNCH!

I WONDER IF THEY'RE HERE TO LOOK FOR BURIED TREASURE..

8-1

THEY HAD CHOCOLATE, STRAWBERRY, AND MARBLE FUDGE, BUT I'M GLAD WE ALL ORDERED VANILLA..

"NO!" THAT'S MY NEW PHILOSOPHY..

8-2

I DON'T CARE WHAT ANYONE SAYS, THE ANSWER IS, "NO!"

THAT'S YOUR NEW PHILOSOPHY, HUH?

YES! I MEAN, "NO!"

YOU RUINED MY NEW PHILOSOPHY..

HARICOT VERT

I'M GOING TO PLAY A TRICK ON MY DOG..

BEFORE I FEED HIM TONIGHT, I'M GOING TO SHOW HIM THIS MENU... WHAT HE WON'T KNOW, IS THAT IT'S ALL IN FRENCH..

THIS IS GOING TO BE SO FUNNY..

GOOD EVENING, SIR.. WOULD YOU LIKE TO SEE OUR MENU?

8-3

HOW DID YOUR TRICK GO? WAS IT FUNNY?

IT WAS KIND OF FUNNY..

HEY, MANAGER...I'M FILING A COMPLAINT WITH THE LEAGUE OFFICE THAT YOU'RE TOO HARD ON YOUR PLAYERS..

WE DON'T HAVE A LEAGUE OFFICE

I FILED IT WITH YOUR CATCHER..

8-4

THIS IS A PRETTY GOOD STORY..

BUT HOW DOES IT FEEL TO KNOW THAT NO MATTER WHAT YOU WRITE, IT WILL NEVER BE AS GOOD AS "WAR AND PEACE"?

DON'T TELL MY MOM..

SCHULZ

HAPPY BIRTHDAY, AMY

8-5

Dear Pen Pal,
Once again I take pen in hand

YOU DROPPED IT..

RATS!

NOW, YOU HAVE TO SAY, "ONCE AGAIN I TAKE PEN IN HAND, BUT I DROPPED IT..SO ONCE MORE I TAKE PEN IN HAND.."

ISN'T THERE SOMETHING ELSE YOU COULD BE DOING?

8/6

SCHULZ

WHY DON'T YOU GET A PEN PAL OF YOUR OWN? THEN YOU WOULDN'T ALWAYS BE BOTHERING ME

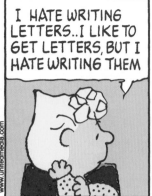
I HATE WRITING LETTERS..I LIKE TO GET LETTERS, BUT I HATE WRITING THEM

MAYBE YOU COULD WRITE THEM FOR ME..

BUT WOULD YOU LET ME READ THE ONES YOU GOT BACK?

ARE YOU KIDDING?!

I DON'T LOOK SO BAD AFTER ALL!

THAT'S ALWAYS BEEN MY AMBITION...

TO NOT LOOK SO BAD AFTER ALL..

WELCOME TO THIS YEAR'S ALL-STAR GAME!

WE ARE PROUD TO ANNOUNCE THAT THIS YEAR WE HAVE TWICE AS MANY PEOPLE WATCHING OUR GAME AS WE HAD LAST YEAR!

LAST YEAR I WAS THE ONLY ONE..

258

THEY SAY, WHEN YOU FALL OFF A HORSE, YOU SHOULD GET RIGHT BACK ON..

STAY WHERE YOU ARE..I'LL GO FIND A HORSE

259

GROUND RULE DOUBLE!

ASK YOUR DAD IF HE WANTS ME TO RAKE YOUR LEAVES..

OUR LEAVES ARE STILL ON THE TREES..

YOU'RE RIGHT..

SHOULD I COME BACK TOMORROW?

I THOUGHT YOU WERE GOING TO MAKE SOME MONEY RAKING LEAVES..

THE LEAVES ARE STILL ON THE TREES..

RAKE 'EM OFF!

260

I THINK I HAVE IT FIGURED OUT..

8-14

FIVE THOUSAND TWO HUNDRED AND EIGHTY TIMES AROUND THE LAKE IS ONE MILE..

NO, IF YOU FALL IN, YOU HAVE TO START OVER..

© 1997 United Feature Syndicate, Inc.

I HAVE A PROBLEM, MARCIE.. I NEED YOUR ADVICE..

I WAS SUPPOSED TO BE GOING TO SUMMER SCHOOL, BUT I FORGOT ALL ABOUT IT..

www.unitedmedia.com

I DON'T KNOW WHAT TO SAY, SIR..I'VE NEVER DONE ANYTHING THAT DUMB...

8-15

WHEN WE GO AWAY TO COLLEGE, MARCIE, LET'S NOT ROOM TOGETHER..

© 1997 United Feature Syndicate, Inc.

IF I GET A BITE, YOU GRAB THE NET..

NOW!

8-16

www.unitedmedia.com

© 1997 United Feature Syndicate, Inc.

261

CLOMP!

AAUGH!

BONK!

MY REGULAR DOG USUALLY LIES ON TOP OF THE DOGHOUSE

YOU HAVE SOME VISITORS OUT FRONT..

DON'T TELL ME...

WE'RE BACK! I THINK WE TOOK A WRONG TURN..

8-18

© 1997 United Feature Syndicate, Inc.

www.unitedmedia.com

YOU GUYS HAVE BEEN WANDERING AROUND FOR THREE MONTHS?!

WE COULDN'T FIND THE DESERT.. WE ENDED UP IN ALASKA...

WE GOT JOBS AS SLED DOGS.. DID YOU KNOW "ROSEBUD" WAS A SLED?

8-19

© 1997 United Feature Syndicate, Inc.

ASK YOUR DOG IF HE WANTS TO COME OUT AND PLAY..

8-20

www.unitedmedia.com

© 1997 United Feature Syndicate, Inc.

THERE'S A STUPID KID OUT FRONT WHO WANTS TO PLAY..

ASK HIM IF HE KNOWS "GO FISH"

HERE YOU GO.. THREE DOGS, THREE SUPPERS!

SUPPERTIME! IT'S SUPPERTIME! YES, IT'S SUPPERTIME!

WHAT WAS THAT ALL ABOUT?

I'M SORRY.. HE KIND OF EXPECTS IT..

EVERY NIGHT? HOW EMBARRASSING

I THINK WE HAVE A PROBLEM..

MY DAD SAYS WE CAN'T AFFORD TO FEED THREE DOGS..

OF COURSE, ONE OF YOUR BROTHERS EATS MORE THAN ALL OF YOU..

WHICH ONE?

WE'VE DECIDED WE SHOULD BE MOVING ON..YOUR FAMILY CAN'T AFFORD THREE DOGS..

WE'LL TRY TO FIND OUR BROTHER SPIKE..HE KNOWS MICKEY MOUSE, WHO IS VERY WEALTHY, AND CAN GET US JOBS IN HOLLYWOOD..

BE CAREFUL CROSSING THE STREET..

And so my brothers Andy and Olaf left to find our brother Spike who lives in the desert.

8-25

I DON'T THINK THAT WAS A DESERT..

THAT KID LOOKED AT ME REAL FUNNY..

IS THERE SOMETHING WRONG WITH US, OLAF? HAVE WE WASTED OUR LIVES?

IT'LL BE DIFFERENT WHEN WE FIND SPIKE, AND HE INTRODUCES US TO MICKEY MOUSE..

MAYBE HE CAN GET US ON SOME TALK SHOWS..

WE CAN'T TALK

MAYBE WE COULD PRETEND WE'RE LITTLE KIDS IN DOG SUITS..

8-26

WE SHOULDN'T HAVE TO BE HIDING IN BARNS, OLAF.. MAYBE WE SHOULD HAVE BEEN HUNTING DOGS..

I CHASED A RABBIT ONCE.. HE JUST LAUGHED AT ME..LATER WE BECAME QUITE GOOD FRIENDS..

8-27

SO! ANOTHER DAY OF WALKING..

8-28

MA! I FOUND A DOG!!

When the little girl caught Andy and took him home, Olaf was left alone.

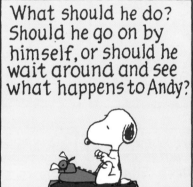

What should he do? Should he go on by himself, or should he wait around and see what happens to Andy?

8-29

THIS WASN'T MY IDEA..

PSST, ANDY! I'VE COME TO HELP YOU ESCAPE..

I CAN'T ESCAPE.. I'M TIED TO A TREE!

8-30

267

PEANUTS *by Schulz*

YES, SIR.. WE'RE HERE TO BUY SCHOOL SUPPLIES..

YOU GO FIRST, MARCIE..

WELL, I'LL NEED A NEW BINDER, SOME PAPER, A SMALL NOTEBOOK, SIX PENCILS, A BALL POINT PEN...

8-31

..A SPELLING DICTIONARY, AN EIGHTEEN-INCH RULER, A PLASTIC TRIANGLE, AND A WORLD MAP..

LUNCH SACKS..

Days turned into weeks.. weeks into months.

We never heard anything more from Andy and Olaf.

I imagine they're still out there somewhere, walking and walking, trying to find their brother Spike in the desert.

IT SAYS, "TO CROSS STREET, PUSH BUTTON"

IT'S PROBABLY SOME KIND OF TRICK..

US MAIL

9-1

I HAVE A NEW PHILOSOPHY.. "WHY ME?"

9-2

DO THIS! DO THAT! WHY ME? GO HERE! GO THERE! WHY ME?

IF YOU'D MOVE A LITTLE BIT, I COULD SEE THE TV...

WHY ME?

SCHOOL STARTS AGAIN NEXT WEEK, RERUN..

I'M NOT GOING.. THE TEACHER HATES ME..

YOUR OLD TEACHER MOVED AWAY..THIS YEAR YOU'LL HAVE A NEW TEACHER..

SHE DOESN'T EVEN KNOW ME, AND ALREADY SHE HATES ME!

9-3

PEANUTS by Schulz

AN ERASER?

AND ON THE FIRST DAY OF SCHOOL..

I DECIDED WE ALL NEED TO SHOW MORE RESPECT.. TO BE MORE CONSIDERATE.. MORE POLITE...

" SO WHEN THE TEACHER CAME IN, I STOOD UP, AND GREETED HER".

GOOD MORNING, MA'AM..

" I LOOKED AROUND, AND I WAS THE ONLY ONE STANDING SO I SAT DOWN.."

" THE TEACHER DIDN'T SAY ANYTHING.. SHE JUST STARED AT ME LIKE MAYBE SHE WAS IN SHOCK..."

9-7

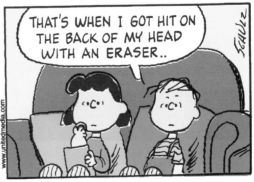

THAT'S WHEN I GOT HIT ON THE BACK OF MY HEAD WITH AN ERASER..

271

YOUR HAIR LOOKS NICE TODAY, SIR..

THANKS, MARCIE.. I WANT TO LOOK MY BEST WHEN THE TEACHER ASKS ME THAT VERY..

9-8

...FIRST QUESTION

HOW WAS SCHOOL TODAY?

I DIDN'T GO..I MEAN, I GOT TO THE FRONT DOOR, BUT I DIDN'T GO IN..

I SAT ON THE STEPS FOR A WHILE..THEN I OPENED THE DOOR...

DOES ANYONE IN THERE NEED ME?!

9-9

NOBODY ANSWERED SO I WENT HOME..

9-10

DIDN'T SCARE ME A BIT..

BIRDS CAN'T SAY, "BOO!"

As she said, "Goodbye" and ran up the steps, he knew he would never see her again.

He was heartbroken.

"Oh, well," he thought. "I still have my dog."

Little did he know, his dog had been planning to leave him.

273

SURE, IT'S ALWAYS ME, ISN'T IT?

ALL RIGHT, IF THAT'S THE WAY EVERYBODY FEELS, I'LL LEAVE!

I KNOW WHEN I'M NOT WANTED! I KNOW WHEN I'M NOT LOVED! I KNOW WHEN EVERYONE IS AGAINST ME!

WHEN?

WHEN?! WHAT DO YOU MEAN, WHEN?!

I MEAN, DID YOU KNOW THE EXACT MOMENT WHEN YOU WEREN'T WANTED, AND NOT LOVED, AND EVERYONE WAS AGAINST YOU?

9-14

OR DID YOU MAYBE HAVE THE FEELING COMING ON LAST WEEK OR LAST MONTH, OR MAYBE...

FOR INSTANCE, I KNEW THE EXACT MOMENT WHEN I WAS OVERDOING IT..

C'MON, MARCIE.. WE NEED THE PRACTICE!

IT'S RAINING, AND I HATE FOOTBALL..

WHAT IF YOU MARRY SOMEBODY WHO LIKES TO GO TO FOOTBALL GAMES?

MY HUSBAND WILL BE VERY WEALTHY AND OWN A LUXURY BOX

9-15

DON'T COUNT ON IT, MARCIE!

© 1997 United Feature Syndicate, Inc.

I'M SORRY I WAS LATE, MA'AM..

9-16

WE HAD A LITTLE TROUBLE AT HOME..

www.unitedmedia.com

OUR KITCHEN WAS FULL OF SQUABBLES..

© 1997 United Feature Syndicate, Inc.

SCHULZ

YES, YOUR HONOR, THIS IS MY CLIENT, ALICE, THE INJURED PARTY, WHO FELL DOWN THE RABBIT-HOLE..

9-17

WE INTEND TO PROVE NEGLIGENCE ON THE PART OF THE PROPERTY OWNER FOR FAILING TO POST A WARNING SIGN BY THE RABBIT-HOLE..

www.unitedmedia.com

© 1997 United Feature Syndicate, Inc.

HOW DID YOUR CASE COME OUT TODAY?

THE JUDGE TOLD ME TO TAKE MY HAT OFF IN THE COURTROOM..

SCHULZ

QUICK, MARCIE..I NEED A PENCIL AND SOME PAPER..

AND I NEED AN ERASER, A PEN AND A RULER..

NO, MA'AM..I'M HER CADDIE..

9-18

YES, MA'AM, I KNOW THE ANSWER, BUT I THINK I'LL KEEP IT TO MYSELF...

I DON'T WANT TO HUMILIATE EVERYONE ELSE BY MAKING THEM FEEL STUPID..I'M SORT OF HUMBLE THAT WAY..

9-19

THE ANSWER IS "TWELVE"

THAT'S WHAT I WAS GOING TO SAY..

THIS IS GOING TO BE A BATTLE, CHUCK! SOME OF US MAY NOT COME OUT ALIVE!

IN THAT CASE, LET'S THINK ABOUT WHO FEEDS THE DOG..

9-20

PEANUTS by SCHULZ

CHARLIE BROWN..

SO WHAT WE'LL DO, SEE, IS I'LL HOLD THE BALL, AND YOU COME RUNNING UP AND KICK IT..

SURE, AND YOU PULL IT AWAY, AND I LAND ON MY BACK AND KILL MYSELF..

NOT NECESSARILY.. PEOPLE CHANGE.. TIMES CHANGE.. YOU CAN FEEL IT IN THE AIR..

I THINK SHE MAY BE RIGHT.. I'VE NOTICED THAT SAME FEELING.. TIMES ARE CHANGING...

THAT MEANS I'M GONNA KICK THAT BALL CLEAR OVER THE BORDER!

9-21

© 1997 United Feature Syndicate, Inc.

ºAAUGH!º

WHERE? WHERE?!

WHUMP!

SORRY, CHARLIE BROWN.. I THOUGHT I HEARD SOMEONE SAY THE MILLENNIUM IS COMING..

www.unitedmedia.com

277

SIR, WHY DO SOME OF YOUR CLUBS WEAR BEDROOM SLIPPERS?

JUST CARRY THE BAG, MARCIE..

YES, SIR..MY DOG NEEDS A NEW SUPPER DISH..

HE WEARS THEM OUT VERY FAST..

NO, I ONLY FEED HIM ONCE A DAY..

PLEASE! JUST PAY HIM, AND LET'S GET OUT OF HERE..

THE MAN AT THE STORE THOUGHT IT WAS VERY FUNNY THAT YOU WEAR OUT SO MANY SUPPER DISHES..

HE SAID HIS DOG HAS HAD THE SAME DISH ALL HIS LIFE..

HE PROBABLY NEVER LICKS THE BOTTOM OF THE DISH..

YES, SIR..WE NEED ANOTHER NEW SUPPER DISH..

THE OTHER ONE DIDN'T LAST LONG..SEE?HE ATE RIGHT THROUGH THE BOTTOM

WE BOUGHT IT HERE YESTERDAY, REMEMBER?

9-25

NO, I THINK HE ATE THE SALES SLIP..

SCHULZ

© 1997 United Feature Syndicate, Inc.

www.unitedmedia.com

MY DAD SAYS WE CAN'T AFFORD TO KEEP BUYING YOU NEW SUPPER DISHES..

HE SAYS HE MAY HAVE TO REMORTGAGE OUR HOUSE AND HIS BARBER SHOP...

www.unitedmedia.com

I DON'T KNOW.. HE MAY JUST BE JOKING..

I CAN'T LAUGH WHILE I'M EATING..

© 1997 United Feature Syndicate, Inc.

9-26

SCHULZ

© 1997 United Feature Syndicate, Inc.

MY BRAND OF FOOTBALL AGGRAVATES YOU, DOESN'T IT, SIR?

www.unitedmedia.com

SCHULZ

9-27

279

LET'S TRY MY SECRET PLAY, SIR..

WE HAVE A SECRET PLAY, CHARLES.. THIS PLAY IS SO SECRET NO ONE HAS EVER HEARD OF IT!

I THINK THEY'D LIKE TO KNOW WHAT OUR SECRET PLAY IS, SIR..

WELL, DON'T TELL THEM!

OH, I'D NEVER DO THAT..

TO ME, A SECRET IS A SECRET! A PERSON SHOULD NEVER TELL A SECRET..

9-28

IT WORKED, SIR! WE BORED THEM RIGHT OUT OF THE GAME..

"I'm a border collie," he said. "I have to be gone a lot. I have to herd sheep."

"Then, go!" she said. "But don't expect me to wait for you!"

He knew he'd never see her again, and he knew there was nothing he could do about it.

THIS IS A GOOD STORY.. DOES IT HAVE A TITLE?

"Border Collies Don't Cry"

IF I WERE YOU, I'D BE TOTALLY ASHAMED TO HAVE SOMEONE SEE ME SITTING AROUND HOLDING A STUPID BLANKET!

AND THAT DOG LYING IN YOUR LAP LOOKS EVEN MORE RIDICULOUS..

I'D BITE HER, BUT I'M FACING THE WRONG WAY..

THE WAY I SEE IT, YOU HAVE TWO CHOICES..

YOU CAN HELP ME WITH MY SPELLING WORDS..

OR YOU CAN TAKE THE BLAME FOR THE INK I SPILLED DOWN THE COLLAR OF THE KID WHO SITS IN FRONT OF ME..

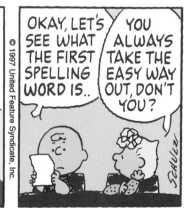
OKAY, LET'S SEE WHAT THE FIRST SPELLING WORD IS..

YOU ALWAYS TAKE THE EASY WAY OUT, DON'T YOU?

281

YES, MA'AM..THAT'S MY DOG OUTSIDE..

WELL, HE DOESN'T LIKE BEING ALONE ALL DAY...

NO, HE'LL JUST WAIT FOR ME OUT THERE ON THE FRONT STEPS..HE'LL FIND SOMETHING TO DO..

10-2

YES, MA'AM...MY DOG IS STILL SITTING OUTSIDE ON THE FRONT STEPS..

NO, I TRIED TO EXPLAIN TO HIM THAT DOGS AREN'T ALLOWED ON THE SCHOOL GROUNDS..

10-3

HERE, HE WANTED ME TO SHOW YOU HIS PASSPORT..

SOMETIMES I LIE AWAKE AT NIGHT, AND I ASK QUESTIONS..

IS THERE ANY ONE THING A PERSON CAN DO TO MAKE HIS LIFE SUCCESSFUL?

"BACK EXERCISES!"

10-4

284

PEANUTS® by Schulz

I ALWAYS DREAD THIS..

OUR VETERINARIAN JUST CALLED..IT'S TIME FOR YOUR CHECKUP..

HE TOOK THE NEWS SURPRISINGLY WELL, DIDN'T HE?

HE DIDN'T TRY TO RUN AWAY OR ANYTHING

I WONDER WHY..

© 1997 United Feature Syndicate, Inc.

www.unitedmedia.com

YES, MA'AM, MY DOG IS HERE TO SEE THE VET..

10-12

HE DIDN'T SEEM AT ALL WORRIED, DID HE?

MAYBE HE'S RECALLED SOME WORDS OF INSPIRATION THAT GIVE HIM STRENGTH..

"HE THAT OUTLIVES THIS DAY, AND COMES SAFE HOME, WILL STAND A-TIPTOE WHEN THIS DAY IS NAMED"

286

HERE, YOU GOT A LETTER FROM YOUR BROTHER SPIKE..

10-13

"DEAR SNOOPY.. WHAT HAPPENED TO ANDY AND OLAF? I THOUGHT THEY WERE COMING OUT HERE.."

"MY FRIEND, MICKEY MOUSE, CAME BY YESTERDAY, AND LEFT THEM SOME GIFTS"

NICE SHOES..

I HATE TO TELL HIM..YOU'D BETTER TELL HIM..

I CAN'T... YOU TELL HIM..

NO, PLEASE..YOU TELL HIM... I DON'T HAVE THE NERVE..

WE THINK MAYBE WE TOOK ANOTHER WRONG TURN..

10-14

ANDY! OLAF! WHAT ARE YOU DOING HERE?

WE COULDN'T FIND THE DESERT..

THAT'S RIDICULOUS!

ACTUALLY, WHAT WE FOUND WAS THE WRONG DESERT..

HAVE YOU EVER SEEN THE PYRAMIDS BY MOONLIGHT?

10-15 SCHULZ

287

And so, Andy and Olaf set off once again to find their brother Spike.

This time, however, I provided them with an experienced guide to show them the way.

10-16

WHAT'S HE SAYING?

10-17

HE SAID THIS IS AS FAR AS WE CAN GO BECAUSE THE EARTH IS FLAT, AND IF WE GO ANY FARTHER, WE'LL FALL OVER THE EDGE..

I WONDER IF HE'S RIGHT..

THERE'S ONLY ONE WAY TO FIND OUT!

OLAF!

HERE, YOU GOT A POST CARD FROM ANDY..

10-18

"DEAR SNOOPY, WE HAD A LITTLE TROUBLE, BUT NOW EVERYTHING IS FINE"

"WILL WRITE MORE LATER"

"P.S. OLAF SAYS TO TELL YOU THE EARTH IS ROUND!"

 HI, CHUCK.. DO YOU MISS ME?

 DO I WHAT?

 MISS ME! DO YOU MISS ME, CHUCK?! WHAT'S THE MATTER WITH YOU? DON'T YOU UNDERSTAND ANYTHING?!

 WHO IS THIS?

10-19

© 1997 United Feature Syndicate, Inc.

 WHAT DO YOU MEAN, WHO IS THIS?! IT'S ME, CHUCK! WHO DID YOU THINK IT WAS?!!

 OH

www.unitedmedia.com

 "OH"? WHAT DOES THAT MEAN? "OH".. IS THAT ALL YOU CAN SAY?!

 I'M SORRY.. I WAS THINKING OF SOMETHING ELSE... I HAVE TO FEED MY DOG..

 WAIT, CHUCK! DON'T HANG UP! SAY SOMETHING! SAY ANYTHING!

 WOOF!

 HOW SWEET!

289

FIGURE SKATING! THAT'S WHERE THE MONEY IS, MARCIE..

10-20

SO WHAT ARE YOU READING?

© 1997 United Feature Syndicate, Inc.

www.unitedmedia.com

"HOW TO DRIVE A ZAMBONI"

SCHULZ

TWENTY-FOUR!

10/21

CHARTREUSE TWENTY-FOUR!

www.unitedmedia.com

© 1997 United Feature Syndicate, Inc.

BETTER IN COLOR, HUH, MA'AM?

SCHULZ

NO, MA'AM, I DON'T HAVE A BLANKET FOR NAP TIME..

MY BROTHER IS THE ONLY ONE IN OUR FAMILY WITH A BLANKET, AND I DON'T WANT TO END UP LIKE HIM..

www.unitedmedia.com

10-22

I'LL JUST SIT HERE AND READ THE PAPER..

© 1997 United Feature Syndicate, Inc.

" '64 CONVERTIBLE.. HARDTOP..BLACK AND RED INTERIOR..$19,000" YOU SHOULD CHECK INTO IT, MA'AM..

SCHULZ

LET'S SAY YOU AND I ARE MARRIED, SEE, AND YOU'RE DOWN IN THE BASEMENT PLAYING YOUR PIANO...

KLUNK!

ALL RIGHT, LET'S SAY YOU'RE OUT IN THE GARAGE PLAYING YOUR PIANO..

10-23

10-24

NOW WHAT?

10-25

THE OTHERS ALL WENT THAT WAY..

WE USED CRAYONS IN SCHOOL TODAY..

WE LEARNED ALL ABOUT COLORS..

LIKE WHAT?

LIKE THE FAT KID NEXT TO ME TAKES ALL THE GOOD COLORS..

10-27

HEY, KID! GIMME YOUR RED CRAYON!

OKAY, I THREW IT INTO THE TEACHER'S WASTEBASKET..IF YOU WANT IT, GO GET IT!

YOU LOOKING FOR A PUNCH IN THE NOSE, KID?

TRY IT, AND I'LL TRADE YOU ONE FOR TWO!

10-28

WELL, MAYBE I LIKE THIS GREEN ONE..

YES, SIR, MR. PRINCIPAL..

WELL, THIS BIG KID WAS TAKING ALL THE CRAYONS, SEE?

THEN HE SAID HE WAS GOING TO PUNCH ME IN THE NOSE..

10-29

HIS MOTHER COMPLAINED ABOUT **ME**?!

SIR? YOU KNOW WHAT I THINK?

YOU AND I SHOULD GO OUT TO DINNER SOMETIME, AND TALK ABOUT THIS..

293

 NO, I CAN'T GO TO SCHOOL.. I'VE BEEN SUSPENDED AGAIN FOR ONE DAY..

 ANOTHER WHOLE DAY!

 YEARS FROM NOW, YOU KNOW WHAT PEOPLE ARE GOING TO SAY ABOUT ME?

 HE'S ONE DAY DUMBER THAN HE SHOULD BE!

 WHERE'S THE BIG KID TODAY? HIS MOTHER TOOK HIM TO ANOTHER SCHOOL..

 THEN WHERE ARE ALL THE CRAYONS?

 I ALWAYS COLOR THE SKY BLUE..

 SOMEDAY DOGS ARE GOING TO LEARN TO FLY..

 WE LEARNED TO SWIM..WHY CAN'T WE LEARN TO FLY?

 I CAN SEE IT NOW.. MILLIONS OF DOGS ALL FLYING SOUTH FOR THE WINTER..

 BEAGLES LEADING THE WAY!

PEANUTS. by SCHULZ

ASK YOUR DOG IF HE WANTS TO COME OUT AND SHOOT A FEW BASKETS..

11-2

© 1997 United Feature Syndicate, Inc.

www.unitedmedia.com

I COULDN'T FIND HIM, BUT I DOUBT IF HE WOULD HAVE BEEN INTERESTED..

SCHULZ

THIS IS GREAT.. I REALLY LIKE IT..

NOW ALL YOU NEED IS A GOOD TITLE..

Ten Stupid Things Dogs Do To Mess Up Their Lives

11-3

I SUPPOSE YOU REALIZE THAT YOUR MAIN JOB HERE IS BEING A WATCHDOG..

11-4

WHAT I'M WONDERING IS, ARE YOU DOING MORE WRITING THAN WATCHING?

IF A BURGLAR COMES AROUND, HAVE HIM STAND RIGHT HERE, AND I'LL DROP A TYPEWRITER ON HIS HEAD..

THERE'S THE HOUSE WHERE THE LITTLE RED-HAIRED GIRL LIVES..

WHEN SHE COMES OUT, I'LL SAY, "GOOD MORNING"

THEN SHE'LL SAY, "WHY ARE YOU STANDING HERE IN THE RAIN?"

11-5

THEN I'LL SAY, "OH, IS IT RAINING?"

THEN SHE'LL SAY, "BOY, ARE YOU EVER STUPID!"

DANCING IN THE RAIN IS ROMANTIC.. STANDING IN THE RAIN BEHIND A TREE ISN'T ROMANTIC..

296

THERE'S A BUNCH OF RABBITS... CHASE 'EM!

11-6

THEY SAID I NEED AN APPOINTMENT

NO, MA'AM.. I DIDN'T GET MY HOMEWORK DONE

WELL, I HAD TO FEED MY DOG, AND TAKE HIM FOR A WALK, AND THEN READ TO HIM..
11-7

YES, MA'AM, I READ TO MY DOG EVERY NIGHT..

..AND I NEVER ASK HIM TO WRITE A BOOK REPORT

SORRY, MA'AM.. THAT JUST SORT OF SLIPPED OUT..

I MIGHT AS WELL TELL YOU NOW...
11-8

AAUGH!

THE SCARIEST WORDS YOU CAN SAY.."I MIGHT AS WELL TELL YOU NOW"

HA! FOOLED YOU, DIDN'T I? TOO QUICK FOR YOU, WASN'T I?

11-9

IT JUST PROVES ONCE AGAIN THAT WE BLANKET HOLDERS ARE INFINITELY SUPERIOR TO YOU ORDINARY TYPES..

CLOMP!

THIS IS A BORDER COLLIE, SEE, AND THESE ARE THE SHEEP HE'S GUARDING..

SUDDENLY, A WOLF COMES, SO THE BORDER COLLIE GETS ON THE PHONE, AND CALLS IN AN AIR STRIKE!

WE'RE SUPPOSED TO BE DOING WATER COLORS OF FLOWERS..

IT ALL TAKES PLACE IN A MEADOW..

EVERY VETERANS DAY I GO OVER TO BILL MAULDIN'S HOUSE..

WE QUAFF A FEW ROOT BEERS..THEN I TELL HIM WHAT HAPPENED YESTERDAY..

I WENT TO A BOOKSTORE TO GET SOMETHING BY ERNIE PYLE.. THEY NEVER HEARD OF HIM..

I DON'T KNOW, BILL.. I JUST DON'T KNOW..

SIR, YOU KNOW I CAN'T GIVE YOU THE ANSWERS..

RATS!

COULD I MAYBE JUST RENT SOME?

Dear Snoopy, I am still waiting for Andy and Olaf to come here.

11-13

"REMEMBER HOW I TOLD YOU THAT MY WEALTHY FRIEND MICKEY MOUSE LEFT SOME SHOES HERE FOR THEM?"

Bad news! Last night somebody stole them!

"IF YOU SEE A COYOTE WEARING MICKEY MOUSE SHOES, GRAB HIM!"

OLAF, HAVE YOU EVER SEEN A COYOTE?

11-14

NOT SINCE I LEFT THE FARM..

I THINK I JUST SAW ONE..

AND HE WAS WEARING MICKEY MOUSE SHOES!

Z

I'VE BEEN THINKING ABOUT SOMETHING..IF I SAW THAT COYOTE WEARING MICKEY MOUSE SHOES, COULDN'T THAT MEAN WE'RE GETTING CLOSE TO WHERE SPIKE LIVES?

I DOUBT IT.. IF WE WERE CLOSE, WE'D KNOW IT BECAUSE WE'RE WELL BRED HUNTING DOGS..

11-15

© 1997 United Feature Syndicate, Inc.

AND IT SAYS," MOSES WAS ON THE MOUNTAIN FORTY DAYS AND FORTY NIGHTS"

THAT'S A LONG TIME TO BE AWAY..

I WONDER WHO HE GOT TO STAY WITH HIS DOG..

Dear Pen Pal, Did you get my last letter?

HOW DOES SHE KNOW IF THE LETTER SHE GOT WAS YOUR LAST LETTER?

AND IF SHE DOESN'T GET THIS LETTER, HOW WILL SHE KNOW YOU ASKED HER IF SHE GOT YOUR LAST LETTER?

? I'D SAY, "THREE NO-TRUMP.."

BUT AFTER THIS HAND, I THINK YOU SHOULD ALL GO TO SLEEP..

305

YOU KICKED THE FOOTBALL UP INTO THE TREE, SIR..

I KNOW HOW TO GET IT DOWN..

YOU STAND IN FRONT OF THE TREE..I'LL RUN UP AND JUMP ON YOUR SHOULDERS...

MY SHOELACE IS UNTIED AGAIN..

11-30-97

© 1988 United Feature Syndicate, Inc.

WHAM!

OKAY, SIR..I'M READY WHEN YOU ARE!

WHAT ARE YOU DOING DOWN THERE?

FORGET IT, MARCIE! IF THE BALL WANTS TO STAY IN THE TREE, LET IT STAY..

WE'LL PROBABLY NEVER MAKE IT TO THE SPLENDID BOWL ANYWAY, SIR

SUPER BOWL, MARCIE!

Dear Brother Snoopy, This year I had a great idea.

For my Christmas tree, I decorated a tumbleweed.

It looked really beautiful.

12-1-97

But then it left!

12-2-97

YES, MA'AM, I'D LIKE TO BUY A CHRISTMAS PRESENT FOR A GIRL I KNOW..

12-3-97

I WAS THINKING MAYBE A PAIR OF GLOVES...

WOULD IT HELP IF I DESCRIBED HER?

WELL, SHE HAS TEN FINGERS..

I WANTED TO BUY PEGGY JEAN SOME GLOVES FOR CHRISTMAS, BUT THEY COST TWENTY-FIVE DOLLARS

SHE'S GOING TO BE DISAPPOINTED WHEN SHE FINDS OUT HER BOYFRIEND IS A CHEAPSKATE

I'M NOT A CHEAPSKATE.. I JUST DON'T HAVE TWENTY-FIVE DOLLARS

PUT IT ON YOUR CREDIT CARD..

I DON'T HAVE A CREDIT CARD..

SO LONG, PEGGY JEAN !

YOU KNOW WHY I WANT TO BUY PEGGY JEAN THOSE GLOVES FOR CHRISTMAS?

WHEN I FIRST MET HER THIS SUMMER AT CAMP, I NOTICED WHAT PRETTY HANDS SHE HAD... I WANT THOSE PRETTY HANDS TO BE WARM..

BUT I DON'T HAVE TWENTY-FIVE DOLLARS TO BUY THE GLOVES...

SEND HER A NICE CARD, AND TELL HER TO KEEP HER HANDS IN HER POCKETS !

SEE? THERE THEY ARE... THOSE ARE THE GLOVES I'D LIKE TO BUY PEGGY JEAN FOR CHRISTMAS..

WHERE ARE YOU GOING TO GET TWENTY-FIVE DOLLARS?

THAT'S THE PROBLEM

MAYBE YOU COULD SELL YOUR DOG...

I TAKE IT BACK.. HE'S PROBABLY ONLY WORTH FIFTY CENTS

© 1988 United Feature Syndicate, Inc.

310

LUCY SAID IF I NEED TWENTY-FIVE DOLLARS TO BUY PEGGY JEAN A CHRISTMAS PRESENT, I SHOULD SELL MY DOG...

WHAT A GREAT IDEA!

THAT'S THE FIRST TIME I'VE EVER SEEN HIM SPILL HIS WATER DISH..

12-8-97

YES, MA'AM ... I'M LOOKING AT THOSE GLOVES AGAIN...

I WISH I COULD GET THEM FOR THIS GIRL I KNOW, BUT I CAN'T AFFORD THEM..

12-9-97

I JUST LIKE TO STAND HERE, AND PRETEND I'M BUYING THEM FOR HER..

SORRY, MA'AM, I DIDN'T REALIZE I WAS FOGGING UP THE GLASS..

GO AHEAD, ASK HIM..

IS THIS THE BUS STOP?

- FOR SALE -
JOE GARAGIOLA
AUTOGRAPHED BASEBALL

MAKE ME AN OFFER

ALL I HAVE IS A DIME.. WILL I GET CHANGE?

DO YOU HAVE A BILLIE JEAN KING?

12-10-97

Panel 1: -FOR SALE- USED COMIC BOOKS

ARE THESE ALL YOU HAVE?

12-11-97

© 1990 United Feature Syndicate, Inc.

YES, MA'AM.. I SOLD MY WHOLE COLLECTION OF COMIC BOOKS..SEE? HERE'S THE MONEY! NOW, I CAN BUY THOSE GLOVES FOR THAT GIRL I LIKE...

BROWNIE CHARLES!

PEGGY JEAN! WHAT ARE YOU DOING HERE?

12-12-97

I'VE BEEN SHOPPING WITH MY MOTHER..LOOK, I JUST BOUGHT THIS NEW PAIR OF GLOVES!

AND DID YOU BUY HER THE GLOVES?

SURE..I SOLD MY WHOLE COMIC BOOK COLLECTION TO GET THE MONEY..

THEN I MET HER IN THE STORE, AND SHE SHOWED ME THE NEW PAIR OF GLOVES SHE'D JUST BOUGHT!

© 1990 United Feature Syndicate, Inc.

SO YOU'RE NOT GOING TO GIVE HER THE PAIR YOU BOUGHT?

WHY GIVE HER SOMETHING SHE ALREADY HAS?!

WELL, AT LEAST THEY DIDN'T GO TO WASTE..

12-13-97

312

WHY DO I HAVE THE FEELING THAT SOMEONE HAS JUST THROWN A SNOWBALL AT ME?

IF THAT SNOWBALL HITS ME, THE PERSON WHO THREW IT IS GOING TO REGRET IT FOR THE REST OF HIS LIFE!

12-14-97

SMART! VERY, VERY SMART!

I DON'T KNOW WHO'S HIDING BEHIND THAT TREE WITH A SNOWBALL...

BUT WHOEVER IT IS BETTER GET RID OF IT BECAUSE IF HE THROWS IT AT ME, I'M GONNA POUND HIM INTO THE GROUND!

12-15-97

DID BEETHOVEN EVER PLAY "JINGLE BELLS"?

12-16-97

HE PROBABLY THOUGHT HE WAS TOO GOOD TO PLAY "JINGLE BELLS"

BONK!

IF I HAD BEEN THERE, I WOULD HAVE SAID, "HEY, LUDWIG, PLAY 'JINGLE BELLS'!"

12-17-97

314

I DON'T THINK YOU'RE THE REAL SANTA CLAUS..

IF YOU'RE THE REAL SANTA, WHERE ARE YOUR HELPERS?

HELP HELP HELP

THAT'S THE DUMBEST THING I'VE EVER SEEN!

WHO CARES? MERRY CHRISTMAS, SWEETIE! WOOF, WOOF, WOOF!

SO THEY ALL GO OFF SHOPPING, AND I'M LEFT ALONE IN THE CAR..

THAT'S OKAY..I'LL JUST SIT HERE AND..

ALL RIGHT, GET THAT TRUCK OUT OF THE WAY! WHERE'D YOU LEARN TO DRIVE, IN A CEMETERY? SAME TO YOU, FELLA!!

..BE THE CHAUFFEUR..

315

"FOUR CALLING BIRDS, AND A PARTRIDGE IN A PEAR TREE.." ♪

THAT SONG DRIVES ME CRAZY!

WHAT IN THE WORLD IS A "CALLING BIRD"?

A CALLING BIRD IS A KIND OF PARTRIDGE..

IN I SAMUEL, 26:20, IT SAYS, "FOR THE KING OF ISRAEL HAS COME OUT TO SEEK MY LIFE JUST AS THOUGH HE WERE HUNTING THE CALLING BIRD.."

THERE'S A PLAY ON WORDS HERE, YOU SEE.. DAVID WAS STANDING ON A MOUNTAIN CALLING, AND HE COMPARED HIMSELF TO A PARTRIDGE BEING HUNTED...

ISN'T THAT FASCINATING?

IF I GET SOCKS AGAIN FOR CHRISTMAS THIS YEAR, I'LL GO EVEN MORE CRAZY!

12-21-97

HAVE I EVER TOLD THE WORLD WAR I FLYING ACE HOW MUCH I ADMIRE HIS BEAUTIFUL SILK SCARF?

PERHAPS THE FLYING ACE MIGHT BE WILLING TO TRADE IT FOR A LITTLE KISS...

12-22-97

THE FAMOUS WORLD WAR I FLYING ACE LOOKS LONELY..

WOULD IT HELP IF I HELD HIS PAW FOR AWHILE?

LIKE MAYBE UNTIL 1918?

12-23-97

HE HAS THESE REINDEER, SEE, AND THEY FLY THROUGH THE AIR PULLING HIS SLED...

AND IF YOU BELIEVE THAT, I HAVE A GOLD BIRD NEST THAT I'LL SELL YOU FOR A DOLLAR!

HA HA HA HA!

MERRY CHRISTMAS, LITTLE FRIEND..

317